WINDOWS XP
TIPS & TRICKS

STUART YARNOLD

In easy steps is an imprint of Computer Step
Southfield Road · Southam
Warwickshire CV47 0FB · United Kingdom
www.ineasysteps.com

Notice of Liability
Every effort has been made to ensure that this book contains accurate and current information. However, Computer Step and the author shall not be liable for any loss or damage suffered by readers as a result of any information contained herein.

Trademarks
Microsoft® and Windows® are registered trademarks of Microsoft Corporation. All other trademarks are acknowledged as belonging to their respective companies.

Printed and bound in the United Kingdom

ISBN 1-84078-297-8

Table of Contents

XP Annoyances 53

Cosmetic Customization 61

Multimedia 77

Security 87

Installation/Setting Up 101

Shortcuts 115

The Internet 125

Email 149

Miscellaneous 165

Index 187

Performance

This chapter covers tips that will enable users to get their PCs running at optimum performance levels.

Covers

Chapter One

Introduction

Windows XP's architecture is based on Windows 2000, which is Microsoft's premier operating system. As such, it is radically different in many ways from Windows 95, 98 and ME. Because of this, many tricks and tweaks that worked with these older systems won't work with XP.

Windows is the most widely used of all the various operating systems on the market and, of these, XP is currently the most popular version.

No other system comes close to matching it in terms of sheer "user friendliness". It's widely available, easy to install/configure and is the most reliable and crash-proof home system Microsoft have yet produced.

One of the main reasons for the enduring popularity of Windows operating systems in general is their "tweakability". They provide the user with an almost limitless number of settings and options, which can be tweaked and adjusted. These can be used to customize the user's operating environment, increase performance levels and set up the PC for specific applications. Most people, though, simply have no idea of the extent to which they can set up their PC to suit their own particular purposes and thus boost the efficiency with which they work.

The aim of this book is to show people what they can, and indeed should, be achieving with their PC. In the following pages you will find a range of categorized tips that, amongst many other things, will enable you to get optimal performance out of your PC, customize the "look" of XP and create a secure working environment.

Security is one of the major issues with Windows XP, the Home edition in particular. In Chapter Seven, you will find many tips to help you increase the security level of your PC and thus avoid the modern plagues of viruses and browser hijackers.

Unfortunately, XP does have some serious security failings that have resulted in users being plagued by viruses and browser hijacking. Chapter Seven gives you the low-down on these issues and how to overcome them.

There are also several features in XP that many people find extremely irritating. These include "unsigned driver" warning messages and "error report" messages that pop up periodically. Getting rid of these is easy – if you know how.

Computers are finely-tuned machines, much like Indy cars, and to keep them running at peak performance levels, they need constant care and attention. Chapter One shows how to achieve this.

Junk mail now accounts for over fifty percent of email traffic worldwide. However, by following a few basic rules, the bulk of it is avoidable; find out how on pages 160–161.

A common use of computers is to access email and the Internet. In Chapters Ten and Eleven we'll see how to get the best out of these popular applications with, for example, tips on how to achieve reliable connections and downloads. Viruses are another aspect of email that need to be considered, and you will learn how to identify potentially dangerous messages before they can damage your computer.

Spam email is rapidly reaching epidemic proportions and we include some useful tips on how to keep the spammers at bay.

Installing and setting up XP isn't always the straightforward procedure it's supposed to be. However, there are things you can do to ensure that XP's installation routine goes without a hitch. Chapter Eight explains how. You'll also learn here how to dual boot (run two separate operating systems on the same machine). This can be very useful in certain situations.

XP provides many ways to improve the efficiency and speed with which you work. Quick access to frequently used applications is one, and Chapter Nine details a number of useful shortcuts that will save you time and effort.

The tips and tricks in this book are designed to work with Windows XP Home Edition. Some will work with other Windows versions, some won't.

The introduction of CD and DVD burners has given multimedia applications a much needed boost, and Chapter Six gives many related tips, including how to create your own DVD movies and get the best out of computer games.

In Chapter Twelve, we have placed a selection of miscellaneous tips ranging from the frivolous (how to cheat at Minesweeper) to more serious stuff, such as how to speed up search engine searches.

All in all, there should be something for everyone here.

Windows XP System Requirements

Windows XP is a powerful and complex piece of software, much more so than the operating systems which preceded it. Each successive version of Windows has introduced new features and technology designed to improve and further the operating system's capabilities. However, this has come at a price – namely the system resources or requirements needed to run it. This is particularly so with XP.

Therefore, before you start trying to improve XP's performance level, you need to ensure that your system is capable of running XP to begin with.

Microsoft's recommended system requirements are:

- Processor speed of 300 MHz
- 128 MB of RAM
- 1.5 GB available hard disk space
- SuperVGA (800 x 600) resolution video card and monitor

The minimum requirements are:

- Processor speed of 233 MHz
- 64 MB of RAM

However, if you try running XP with these minimum requirements or less, you will find that its performance level will be severely impaired. It will run but you won't find it a happy experience.

The most important of these requirements is RAM (memory). At the moment RAM is cheap (it is also very easy to install), so if your PC is lacking in this department, upgrade it. Some applications will require a minimum of 256 MB of RAM to function properly.

Processors are a slightly different matter as upgrading these often necessitates a motherboard upgrade as well. However, in order to get the best out of XP, this may be necessary.

To sum up, XP will not perform well in a low-specified machine, just as a Model T Ford wouldn't, even if fitted with an Indy car engine. It needs suitable hardware to support it.

If, after installing XP, you discover it doesn't perform as well as you expected, take a look at how much memory your system has. If it's lower than 128 MB then this will almost certainly be the reason.

Contact the manufacturer of your PC and ask exactly what type of memory module is installed in the PC. Then, armed with this information, take a trip to your nearest computer hardware store and buy some more memory. Then all you have to do is open up the case and plug it in.

Alternatively, disconnect all the peripherals (monitor, keyboard printer, etc.) and take the case into the store with you. With a bit of luck they might install the new memory for you on the spot.

How to Back Up the Registry

The Registry is a central hierarchical database in Windows that holds all of the important Windows settings regarding software, hardware and system configuration, and it provides a common location for all applications to save their launching parameters and data. It contains two main files – "system.dat" and "user.dat." User-specific information is contained in the user.dat file and computer and hardware specific information in the system.dat file.

Injudicious changes to the Registry can have dire consequences, and as many of the tips in this book do involve altering registry settings, it is essential for users to first create a backup copy of the Registry in case things go wrong. Do this as follows:

Before making any changes to the Registry, make a backup copy. In the event of any problems resulting from those changes, you will be able to "undo" them.

If you do forget though, there is always System Restore. This provides an alternative method of restoring your system to a previous state.

1 Go to Start and Run. In the Run box type regedit. This will open the Registry Editor as shown below

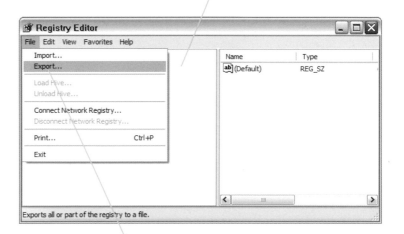

2 On the File menu, click Export. In the Export Registry File dialog box, name the file (Registry Backup, etc.) and save it to a location of your choice

Should you ever need to restore the Registry, just double-click the backup file and it will automatically replace the existing Registry.

Registry Backup

Streamline the Registry

Registry cleaners downloaded from the Internet usually come with restrictions. While they will find the problems, typically, they won't repair them all. To gain the program's full functionality, you will have to buy it.

Over time, the Registry becomes bloated with obsolete and invalid key information, and as these invalid items build up, the effect is degradation of system performance.

The solution is to scan it periodically with a suitable application that will locate all the invalid entries and delete them.

While XP's Registry Editor is adequate for editing purposes, it does not provide a cleaning option. However, there are many of these applications available for download from the Internet. A typical example is "Registry Mechanic" (shown below). These programs provide various options, such as full or selective scans, backups, the creation of System Restore points, etc.

RegClean is a free registry cleaner from Microsoft (although it is no longer supported by them). This is freely available on the Internet. It is a rather basic application, however, and there are many better programs of its type. But it's a good option if you don't want to spend any money.

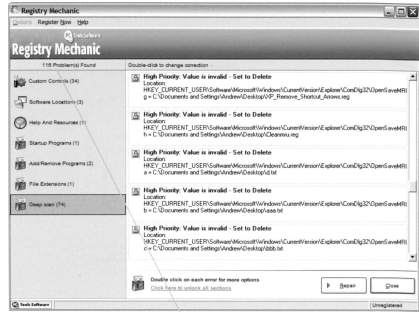

This scan on the author's system has found 116 problems

Regular use of a Registry cleaner will keep your Registry lean and mean, which will result in a faster and more responsive PC.

Defragment the Hard Drive

Fragmentation is a term used to describe the process whereby files saved to a magnetic disk drive have their data split up on different parts of the disk instead of being stored contiguously. When a fragmented file is accessed, the drive's read/write heads have to hunt about to locate all the different parts of the file before they can be reassembled in the original form. The result is that the file will take much longer to open than it should do, and the system as a whole will be sluggish.

To redress this situation, Windows supplies a tool called "Disk Defragmenter", which "undoes" the fragmentation by rearranging the data on the disk so that each file is stored as a complete unit.

Access and use Disk Defragmenter as follows:

1 Go to Start, All Programs, Accessories, System Tools

2 Select a drive, then click Defragment

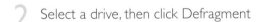

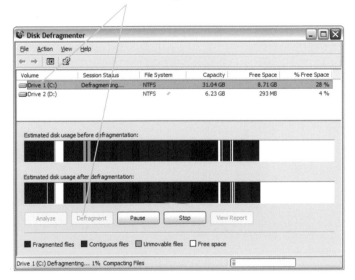

Disk Defragmenter can also be used on other types of magnetic disk such as Floppy and Zip disks. It is good practice to run it on your hard drive at least once a month. To make this a bit easier, you can set the program to run automatically by using XP's Scheduled Task Wizard (also accessible from System Tools).

Adjust XP's Display Properties

There can't be many computer users these days that aren't aware that they can right-click on an empty area of the Desktop, click Properties and then the Appearance tab, to have access to a whole range of display tweaks.

Windows XP, however, gives you even more. Click Start, Control Panel, System, Advanced, Performance, Settings. This opens Visual Effects in Performance Options. Here you have a whole range of further options:

In general, Windows operating systems provide a large number of special effects. XP is even more generous in this respect and provides scrolling menus, fade-out menus, shadows, font smoothing, and animation, etc.

However, they all consume system resources, and the more you enable, the fewer resources you will have available for more important things.

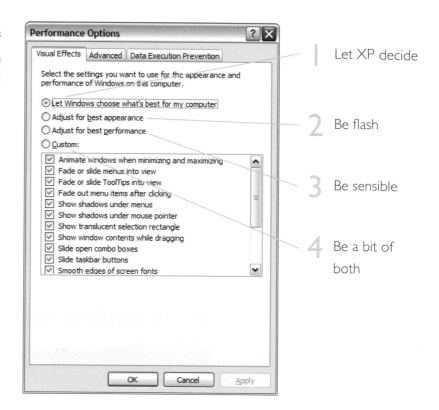

1 Let XP decide

2 Be flash

3 Be sensible

4 Be a bit of both

Unfortunately, the more of these display effects you enable, the more the system resources needed to run them. Obviously, if you have a highly-specified machine you needn't worry too much, but if you are looking to speed up the system wherever possible, then this is one area where worthwhile performance gains can be made.

Disable Unneeded Internal Services

The following Services can be turned off without any ill effect, unless you are using the computer for networking:

- Alerter
- Clipbook
- Computer Browser
- Fast User Switching
- Indexing Service
- Messenger
- Net Logon
- NetMeeting Remote Desktop Sharing
- Remote Desktop Help Session Manager
- Remote Registry
- Routing & Remote Access
- Server
- SSDP Discovery Service
- TCP/IP NetBIOS Helper
- Telnet
- Device Host
- Upload Manager
- Wireless Zero Configuration
- Workstation

When a computer is being used, in the background, and unseen by the user, a number of applications known as Services will be running. These are managed automatically by XP, and generally, it does this well. However, there are times when XP gets it wrong and runs Services that aren't actually required. As every open application takes its toll on system performance, this is something you do not want to be happening. Fortunately, you can override XP and make the decision yourself as to which ones should be running. Do it as follows:

1 Go to Start, Control Panel, Administrative Tools. Then click Services

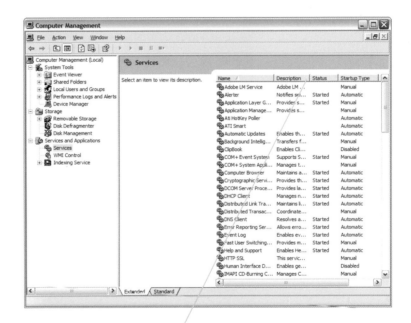

2 Use these tabs as described in the table below:

Description	Tells you what a particular Service does
Status	Lets you know if a Service is running or not
Startup type	Tells you if the Service starts manually or automatically

The Indexing Service creates and constantly updates an index of all the files in the computer. The purpose of this is to speed up file searches. However, it is a serious drain on the system's resources, and so disabling it will improve the system's overall performance. It will only be of benefit if you do a lot of file searching.

The Dependencies tab is important as it gives you forewarning of what will happen if you stop a particular Service. For this reason, it is well worth having a good look here prior to making any changes.

Generally, if a Service is set to run automatically by default, it's because XP thinks it will need it. However, XP isn't always right, and if you know for sure that you don't require a particular Service, then override XP and set it to manual. Be aware that this doesn't permanently disable the Service; it simply means that it won't run until definitely needed, in which case XP will start it. If it genuinely isn't required, however, then it won't run, saving you system resources.

A guide to the importance of a Service can be obtained by right-clicking it, which will open its Properties window:

| Description of the service

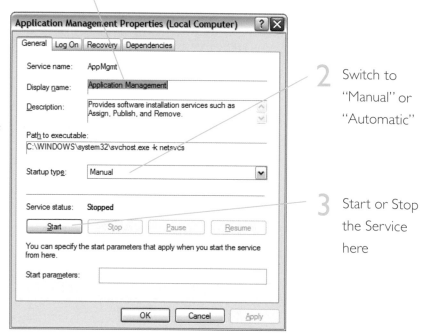

2 Switch to "Manual" or "Automatic"

3 Start or Stop the Service here

4 In the Dependencies dialog box, you can see what the effect of turning a particular Service off will be. For example, there may be other system components dependent on it. Alternatively, there may be other components on which the Service is itself dependent.

Run XP From Memory

The heart or core of XP is its kernel. The kernel is responsible for managing memory, handling device signals, task scheduling, and other essential tasks. It is one of the first components loaded into memory during the boot process, and remains active as long as the computer is operational.

This tweak is only suitable for systems with a minimum of 512 MB of RAM. If it is done on systems with less, when a memory intensive application is run (video-editing, CAD, etc.), performance could be adversely affected.

This tweak prevents XP from paging its kernel to the Page file (also known as virtual memory) and forces it to be kept in RAM. The advantage of this is that because RAM operates a lot faster than the hard drive (where the page file is located), system performance is much improved.

Note that you must have at least 512 MB of RAM in your system (see margin note) for this to be effective.

1   Go to Start, Run. In the Run box, type regedit and click OK

2   The Registry Editor will open. Using the hierarchal tree at the left, locate the following key:
     HKEY_LOCAL_MACHINE\System\ControlSet001\Control\
     Session Manager\Memory Management

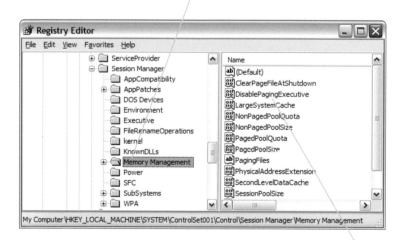

3   Click the Memory Management folder and on the right, double-click DisablePagingExecutive. In the Value Data box, change the 0 to 1. Then close the Registry Editor and reboot

Give Important Programs Priority

"Priority" is the measure that Windows uses to determine the share of processor time that each application receives. By default, most applications are set to the "Normal" priority level, so by changing a specific program to a higher level, you can boost its performance, especially when you are using other applications at the same time (multitasking).

Do the following:

1   Open the program you wish to prioritize

2   Press CTRL+ALT+DEL to open the Task Manager

By increasing the priority level of a program, you are increasing the attention the CPU will give it. This will substantially increase the program's performance.

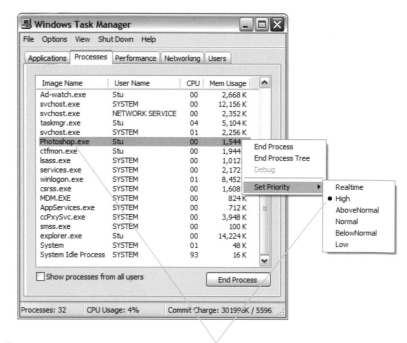

You can also set lower priority levels for your applications. For example, if you have a program running in the background that is accessed infrequently, giving it a lower priority will enable the CPU to allot more resources to the more frequently used programs.

3   Click the Processes tab, locate your application (Photoshop in the example above), right-click it and select the appropriate Priority

One thing to be aware of is that changes to priority level are not permanent. They are only effective while the program is running; if you close it down and then open it again, it will have reverted to the default (Normal) setting.

Force XP to Unload DLL Files

A Dynamic Link Library (DLL) is a special file which contains commonly used instructions that are employed by many different programs. When a DLL is used by a program, XP will cache it in the system memory so it can be accessed quickly when required.

However, XP keeps these DLLs in the memory after the program has been closed, and are thus no longer required. Over a period, as many programs are opened and closed, these DLLs occupy more and more of the RAM's storage space with the result that less is available to programs that need it. At this point, system performance starts slowing down dramatically.

To prevent this, force XP to unload DLLs by doing the following:

1. Open the Registry Editor by typing regedit in the Start Menu Run box.

2. Locate the following key:
HKEY_LOCAL_MACHINE\Software\Microsoft\Windows\CurrentVersion\Explorer

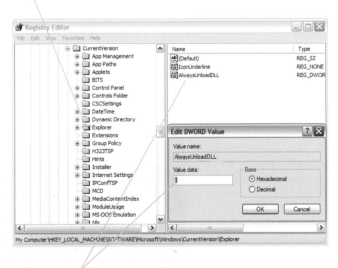

3. Click the Explorer folder, right-click in the right-hand window and create a new DWORD value. Name it: AlwaysUnloadDLL. Double-click this, and in the Value data box, enter 1. Reboot

Boost the System with NTFS

XP provides two file systems – FAT and NTFS. When XP is installed on a system, the user is given the choice of formatting the hard drive with either of these systems. Of the two, NTFS is the better option, as not only is it a faster file system, it also provides more features, such as a higher level of security.

The only situation in which you should use the FAT file system is when you are using XP's dual boot feature to run two or more operating systems (see page 107).

Check which file system your hard drive is using as follows:

1. Open My Computer and right-click the hard drive. Then click Properties. In the Properties dialog box, you will see its file system

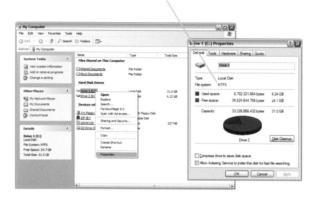

If it's FAT, convert it to NTFS by doing the following:

In the example opposite, the C drive (C:) is being converted. If the drive you want to convert has a different letter, i.e. D, you would type: Convert d: /fs:ntfs

2. Open a command prompt window by going to Start, Run and typing cmd in the Run box. In the command prompt window, type: "Convert c: /fs:ntfs". Hit Enter and the conversion will take place

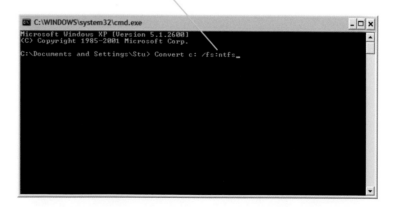

Keep the File System Healthy

Over time, especially if the PC is well used, a multitude of file system and data faults will build up on the hard drive. These can make a serious hit on system performance, and may result in the loss of data.

To correct these types of fault, XP provides a disk checking utility called Chkdsk. Use it as follows:

Make a point of running Chkdsk on a regular basis (once a week is not too often). You can also make use of XP's Scheduled Tasks Wizard (Start, All Programs, Accessories, System Tools) to do the job automatically.

In particular, be sure to run Chkdsk after every incorrect shutdown or system crash. These are events that will introduce file system errors to the hard drive.

1 Open My Computer and right-click the hard drive. Then click Properties and the Tools tab

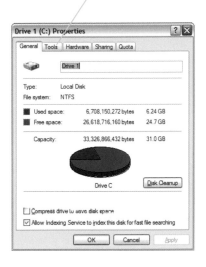

2 Click Check Now

If the drive being checked is the one on which XP is installed, it will be necessary to reboot for the disk check to take place. Any other drive, however, will be checked immediately.

3 In the Check Disk Drive dialog box, tick "Automatically fix file system errors" and "Scan for and attempt recovery of bad sectors"

Reboot the PC, and on restart Chkdsk will check the hard drive and repair any faults it finds.

Slim Down the Hard Drive

A hard drive that's approaching its full capacity will reduce system performance.

This is particularly so if the drive is also heavily fragmented – see page 13.

When seventy percent (approximately) of a hard drive's total storage capacity has been exceeded, its performance level starts dropping off. So to make sure it's operating at its optimum, you need to monitor its usage. You can do this by right-clicking the drive in My Computer and clicking Properties.

When it begins to approach the seventy percent mark, you need to start clearing it out.

Basically, all you have to do is delete all unnecessary files. Do this with XP's Disk Cleanup utility as described below:

You can also go through your hard drive and look for programs you no longer use. A good way of doing this is with XP's Add or Remove Programs utility. You will find this in the Control Panel. Running it will show you a list of all the programs installed on the PC. Select the ones you no longer use and simply click the Change/Remove button.

1 Go to Start, All Programs, Accessories, System Tools, Disk Cleanup

2 All these files can be safely deleted. Keep the ones you want and delete the rest

3 Click the More Options tab

System Restore points can take up Gigabytes of disk space. If you are running short, this is the place to start.

Note that, by default, XP reserves 12% of the hard disk for Restore Points. However, you can override this manually. Go to Start, Control Panel, and System. Click the System Restore tab and then click Settings. Drag the slider down to reduce the amount of disk space available to System Restore.

4 Click here to delete all System Restore points except the most recent

Clean Out the Prefetch Folder

Prefetching is basically XP trying to predict what you need before you need it. The first time you run a program, XP's prefetcher copies part of it to the Prefetch folder. Thus, the next time you run the program, XP has the necessary files immediately at hand so that the program loads more quickly. That's the theory, and it does work – up to a point. If you frequently use certain applications, prefetching can greatly increase the speed with which they open.

The drawback is that XP will continue to prefetch any program in the Prefetch folder even if it's been used only once. Over time, as the folder fills up with a large number of applications, it will slow the system down.

The solution is to periodically clean out this folder, which can be found in the Windows folder.

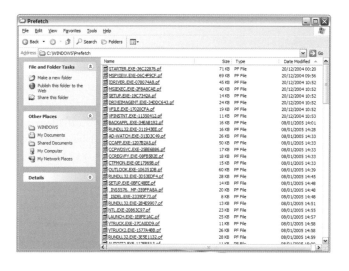

Once a program has been deleted from the Prefetch folder, the next time you run it, it will open much slower than before. However, running it will place it back in the Prefetch folder, and from now on it will open quickly again.

Simply click Edit, Select All, and Delete. Note that when you do this, the next time you run one of the deleted programs, it will not open as quickly as before. Once it is back in the Prefetch folder, however, it will.

The system as a whole will benefit from doing this – boot-up speed in particular, as the system will now no longer have to wait for dozens of programs to be prefetched.

Resource-Hungry Programs

Very few applications over-tax a computer system (games and graphic applications are two exceptions). However, the programs mentioned below can have a serious impact on a system's performance.

Anti-virus Programs

These programs, by necessity, must check everything that is going on in a computer system, and as a result will slow the system down enormously.

Quite apart from their negative impact on system performance, anti-virus programs can also be extremely irritating in the way they often throw up unnecessary and misleading warning messages.

If you use the Internet a lot, particularly with an "always-on" broadband connection, unfortunately, you really do need an anti-virus program to monitor what's coming into the PC. However, if you install XP Service Pack 2 (see page 88) the risks of picking up a virus are much reduced. In this case you may consider just running the anti-virus program when a download or email comes in, checking it and then turning it off again. By not having it running continuously, your system will be much quicker.

Utility Programs

Utility programs are third-party software that offer various functions to a user (system diagnostics, repair, tuning, maintenance, etc.). Probably the best known of these is Norton Utilities, which offers all these, plus many more. Other examples include First Aid and Nuts & Bolts.

Many of the functions offered by utility programs, Norton Speed Start (Norton's version of Microsoft's Disk Defragmenter) being an example, are superior to the tools bundled with Windows. Use these by all means; just avoid the system and hard drive monitoring tools that run permanently in the background.

The one thing that all these programs have in common is that they are resource-hungry. Many of the functions can be run as needed and then turned off when finished with, which isn't too bad. Others, however, such as Norton Disk Doctor, which runs permanently in the background monitoring what's going on in the PC, can be a real drain on system resources and will make a serious hit on the system's performance.

If you decide to make use of this type of software, try to avoid the applications which run in the background, and instead, just use those that can be run when needed and then turned off.

Purge the System of Malware

Malware is a term that encompasses the following:

- Spyware – these programs send information regarding web sites visited, installed programs, contents of the email address book, passwords, credit card numbers, etc

- Adware – these place advertisements on your screen, usually in the form of pop-up windows. If you are browsing, they will often be related to the web page's content

- Hijackers – these take control of your web browser and redirect it to advertisement-related sites

- Toolbars – these are Internet Explorer plug-ins, and if used will direct you to advertisement-related sites

- Dialers – dialers connect your modem to a premium rate number that will saddle you with a hefty phone bill

The vast majority of these programs are bundled with "Freeware" and "Shareware" applications downloaded from the Internet. Also, the file-sharing networks (Kazaa, Grokster, etc,) are rife with them. Simply opening a web page in certain sites will also trigger an unwelcome download.

As these programs are not actually viruses, anti-virus programs are largely ineffective at intercepting them. Once on a user's system, they can be very difficult, and in worst case scenarios, impossible to remove. There are literally thousands of malware programs, and it is common these days for a computer system to be infected with dozens of them.

Malware programs are usually poorly written and can thus render a system extremely unstable. If you have several malware programs installed, they will often conflict with each other and cause even more problems. Even the fastest computer can be brought to its knees with only a handful of malware programs installed.

So, how do you discover if you have malware on your machine? The answer to this is to run an application such as Lavasoft's "Ad-Aware." This is a program designed specifically to hunt out and remove malware applications.

If you are unfortunate enough to be hit with the "CoolWebSearch" browser hijacker, you could be in big trouble. This nasty program has many different names and strains and can be almost impossible to remove. Often a complete clean reinstallation of the operating system is required. Before you do this though, try downloading and running a program called "CoolWebShredder." This program has been written specifically to counter the CoolWebSearch trojan and will often succeed in removing it. However, as CoolWebSearch is updated on an almost weekly basis, success is not guaranteed. You can find CoolWebShredder at www. spywareinfo.com.

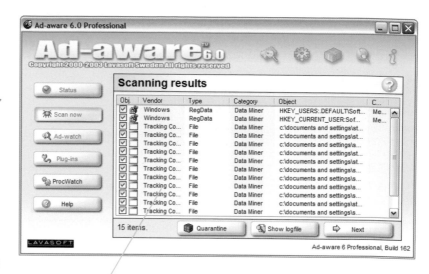

Scan your system with Ad-Aware and you will almost certainly see a load of Malware. Click Next and Ad-Aware will remove them from your system

Unfortunately, no malware-removal program is perfect and some will inevitably slip through the net. Also, many malware programs are so deviously written that Ad-Aware will be unable to remove them; hijackers in particular. So the next step is to download and run "Spybot Search and Destroy," available as a free download at www.safer-networking.org. This program will find malware that Ad-Aware doesn't.

Keep your system "clean" by installing XP Service Pack 2 (this will stop browser hijackers such as CoolWebSearch), and by never running programs downloaded from the Internet.

However, even Spybot will not find them all, so after running both of these programs, you are still likely to have malware on your system. You will, though, have purged it of the vast majority, to the extent that what's left will probably have no noticeable impact on system performance.

The only way guaranteed to purge your system completely, is to do a clean installation of XP as described on page 103.

To prevent a clean system becoming infected by malware, never install Freeware and Shareware software downloaded from the Internet, never install software obtained via file-sharing networks and install XP Service Pack 2 on your system.

Spring-Clean the PC

Formatting your hard drive will literally wipe it clean. You will lose all the data it contained. Before you do this make sure you have backed up everything that you don't wish to lose. There will not be a second chance.

There comes a time in the life of any well-used computer when it will benefit hugely from a good clear out. Over time, as files are saved and deleted, programs installed and uninstalled, the inevitable crashes occur and users do things they shouldn't, a PC will become literally clogged up with redundant and useless data, long forgotten files, broken shortcuts, etc. Also, essential system or program files may go missing or become corrupted, leading to all manner of niggling little faults and problems.

There is absolutely nothing that can be done about this, no matter how much care you take; it is as inevitable as night following day.

So what's the answer? In short, scrap the lot and start again from scratch. This doesn't mean throwing away the computer and buying a new one, but rather junking all the data that's inside it, i.e. on the hard drive.

The method of doing this is known as "formatting" and this procedure will purge the hard drive of all its data. Then, you install a new copy of the operating system, and finally, install new copies of all your programs. The result will be a PC that is, to all intents and purposes, "brand-new." Instead of chugging and spluttering along, it will now roar, much as an old car will if fitted with a new engine.

When doing a Windows installation, it's always better to install to a newly formatted drive. In this way you can be sure of an error-free installation.

In the past, this issue of formatting and "clean" installations has been too intimidating for most users to attempt, involving as it does, Startup disks and DOS prompts.

XP, however, has simplified the whole procedure to the extent that anyone can now do it. All the necessary tools are on the installation disk.

To do it, follow the procedure described on page 106.

Before you do, however, you should make backups of all your data and settings. Things to include are your email messages, email address book, Internet Favorites, passwords, and important data such as documents and graphics.

To assist in making your backups, XP provides you with two tools – the File and Settings Transfer Wizard (see page 111) and its Backup utility (see page 172).

At the end of it, your PC will be like a brand-new machine.

With a well-used computer, this procedure is worth doing every six months or so.

Use Task Manager for a Faster PC

Task Manager is the place to go when you want to discover how much memory your applications are using.

When a computer becomes sluggish and unresponsive, the cause is usually lack of memory. Try this tip to claim some back quickly.

1 Press CTRL+ALT+DEL to open the Task Manager

Although it's much less common with XP, programs will still occasionally "freeze" or "lock-up." Task Manager provides the solution; simply highlight the offending application and click End Task. It won't always be able to do it immediately, so give it a bit of time. In the event that it is unable to close the program, then you will have to resort to the Reset or Power Off button.

2 Click the Processes tab and look at the Mem Usage column. This tells you how much memory an application is using

XP's new improved Task Manager is actually much more worthy of the name than its predecessors. Apart from the applications already mentioned on this page, it will also let you open and close programs, switch between running programs, monitor CPU usage and logoff.

3 If you see a program using an abnormally large amount of memory, you have tracked down the culprit

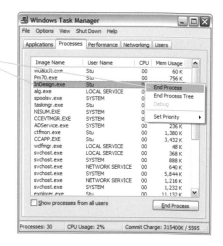

4 Right-click the offending application and then click End Process. Ignore the warning message and click Yes. The program will now be terminated and the memory it was using will be released

Boot-up and Shutdown

Computers that take an eternity to boot-up and shutdown can be a major aggravation. There are, however, several things that can be done to speed up these procedures.

Covers

Chapter Two

Boot-up Tweaks

A new Windows installation will boot extremely quickly. However, over time, this will gradually take longer and longer. The process will not be obviously noticeable as it occurs so slowly. The day will come though, when it suddenly hits the user just how slow the PC's boot-up has become. There are various reasons for this behavior, which we will cover in the next few pages. Generally, however, the problem is the result of simply using the PC, the act of which will inevitably alter the ideal setup of any new computer.

Numerous consumer surveys have shown that one of the things that PC users want most is a fast boot-up. The following pages will show you how to achieve the maximum boot-up speed possible.

Startup Programs

These are applications which open automatically when Windows starts. These programs are located, you won't be surprised to learn, in the Startup folder. Items can be placed here by the user if he or she wants them to open with Windows, so they are ready for immediate use. The problem is that the more programs there are in this folder, the longer the PC will take to boot-up.

Check what's in your Startup folder as follows:

1 Go to Start, All Programs and highlight Startup. This reveals the contents of the Startup folder without actually opening it

2 This menu indicates which programs will start automatically with Windows

Another way of discovering which programs are in the Startup folder is via "System Information." This is accessible from Start, All Programs, Accessories, and System Tools. You will also find a lot of other information about your system here.

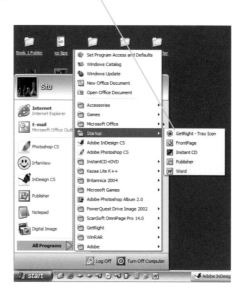

3 Remove any unnecessary entries by right-clicking and then clicking Delete

Be aware that viruses and worms have a habit of disguising themselves with authoritative sounding Windows system file names. For example, the Win32.spybot.worm showed up as MSCONFIG32.EXE.

However, clearing out the Startup folder is only half the battle. You now have to find and get rid of the startup programs that run in the background, and thus aren't so obvious. Most of these are innocuous and do nothing more than slow down the boot procedure. Others, however, can be spyware and viruses, which can seriously affect the performance of a computer. Check this out as follows:

1 Go to Start, Run. In the Run box, type msconfig. This opens the System Configuration Utility. Click the Startup tab

In the screenshot opposite, you will see an entry called "Save." This is a particularly irritating application that opens a new browser window whenever you search for something on the Internet. In this window will be a list of advertisers offering products relating to your search. For example, if your search includes the term "finance," you will be regaled by a list of loan sharks. Quite apart from the irritant factor, this program, and others of its ilk, steals your bandwidth and thus slows down your browser.

These types of program are commonly attached to legitimate programs downloaded from the Internet. When running downloaded programs, always check the Startup folder to see if they have placed anything in it.

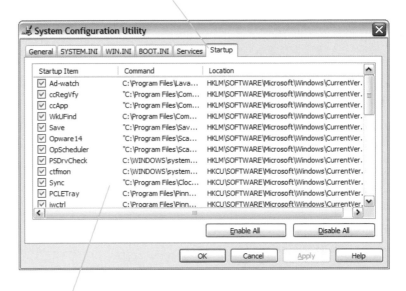

2 Here you will see a list of all the programs that start with Windows and it may come as a bit of a surprise

By removing the tick, you can disable anything you don't like the look of. In fact you can quite safely disable all of them by clicking the Disable All button – none of them play any critical role in the computer. The one exception to this is your anti-virus program.

If you want to find out what any of these programs are (it's not always obvious), go to www.sysinfo.org. Here you will find a huge list of applications which start with Windows.

If you do decide to delete any fonts from the Fonts folder, be sure you do not delete any of the Windows default fonts.

Streamline the Fonts Folder

Windows XP comes with a large number of fonts, which are installed in the Fonts folder. This folder can be accessed by going to My Computer, Control Panel, Fonts. Many other programs, such as Desktop Publishing applications, will also install their own fonts. Over a period, probably unwittingly, you will build up a large collection. As XP checks and loads each of these fonts on boot-up, the more you have, the longer boot-up takes to complete.

The solution is to delete all but the ones used by the system, and the ones you yourself are likely to use. Do it as follows:

1 First, create a backup folder. Then open the Fonts folder in the Control Panel

System fonts can be identified by the date stamp (right-click the file and then click Properties). These dates will be the same as the other Windows system files.

 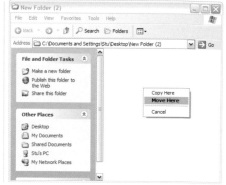

2 With both folders open as shown above, move all the fonts to the backup folder. Within a few seconds Windows will automatically reinstall essential system fonts into the Fonts folder

3 Then go through the fonts in the backup folder, pick out the ones you are likely to use and move them back to the Fonts folder. The rest you can leave in the backup folder where they will always be available should you subsequently find a use for them

Without dozens and dozens of fonts to load, boot-up will now be a lot quicker.

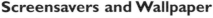

...cont'd

Screensavers and Wallpaper

Back in Neanderthal times, computer monitors were prone to having an impression literally burnt into the screen by prolonged exposure to a static image. To guard against this unfortunate tendency, screensavers were invented. Quite apart from serving a useful purpose, they could also be fun.

These days, however, that's all they are – fun. They are now actually completely superfluous in the modern computer system, as monitors are no longer susceptible to damage caused by static images.

Unless you particularly enjoy watching bouncing balls, fish swimming across your desktop and the like, all you are doing by running them on your system is actually slowing it down. This applies particularly to 3D screensavers.

Wallpapers are quite large bitmap image files that have no function other than to make your Desktop look pretty. They do, however, slow down the boot-up procedure considerably.

You can either disable your screensavers by right-clicking the Desktop and then clicking Properties, Screen Saver, or get rid of them altogether. Do this by opening the Windows folder and looking for a folder called "System 32." Inside this folder you will find all the screensavers installed on your system. To help you identify them, they are all prefaced by "ss" followed by the name of the screensaver, e.g. "sspipes." Simply delete any that you don't want.

To find your Wallpaper files, again, open the Windows folder and scroll down until you find the images, which you will recognize by their names (Coffee Bean, Soap Bubbles, etc.). They can also be identified by their icon which is the same as the Windows Picture and Fax Viewer icon. More wallpaper files can be found by scrolling down to the Web folder; inside this will be another folder called Wallpaper.

Another way to easily locate your wallpaper files is to set the Folder view in the above mentioned folders to Thumbnails. This will give you an instantly recognizable graphical representation of the files.

Screensavers are notorious for causing system crashes. With XP, this is less of a problem due to its inherent stability, but it can be a problem on older versions of Windows.

Graphic files take longer to load than any other software element. If you have a highly-specified machine, this won't matter too much; the PC will be able to handle them. However, if you want to make it as fast as possible, getting rid of as many graphics as you can will give you a significant performance boost.

Change the BIOS Boot Sequence

An easy and effective way of speeding up the boot process is to change the boot sequence in the BIOS. By altering this sequence so that the hard drive is the first device the computer attempts to boot from, you save the few seconds needed for the BIOS to check other devices for bootable media. Do it as follows:

Having changed the BIOS boot sequence, if you subsequently wish to boot the system from a CD or run a floppy disk, you will need to change it again. However, the need to boot from a CD is rare, and most people don't use floppy drives at all anymore, so this shouldn't be a problem.

1 Boot the PC, and on the first boot screen hit the key needed to enter the BIOS Setup program. This will be specified at the bottom of the screen; often it is the Delete key

2 Open the Advanced BIOS Features page using the arrow keys and hit Enter

Regardless of how the BIOS boot sequence has been configured, the BIOS will still attempt to access the floppy drive. To prevent this it will be necessary to disable "Floppy Drive Seek" – see page 35.

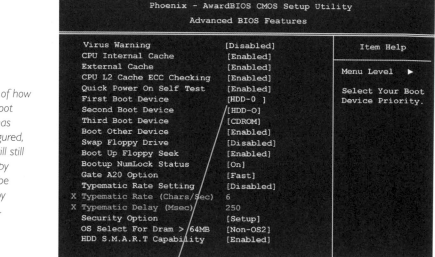

3 Scroll down to First Boot Device, and using the Page Up/Page Down keys, select HDD-0

The only drawback with doing this is that every time you want to use a floppy disk, you will need to reset the boot device to the floppy drive.

Enable Quick Power On Self Test (POST)

This setting has various names depending on the motherboard. Examples are: "perform quick memory test," "quick boot," "quick power on self test," etc.

Every BIOS has an inbuilt diagnostic utility called the Power On Self Test (POST), which checks that vital parts of the system, such as the video and memory, are functioning correctly as the PC is booting up. However, this takes time and serves no practical purpose other than to give an indication of any problem devices. Many motherboards have a setting that will instruct the BIOS to skip through certain parts of the POST, thus speeding up boot times considerably.

1 Enter the BIOS Setup program as described on page 34 and open the Advanced BIOS Features page

2 Scroll down to Quick Power On Self Test and select Enabled

Amongst other things, this will make the BIOS skip the memory count that occurs when you turn on your PC. It's a very basic memory test and the chances are, if you really do have bad memory, the test won't catch it anyway.

Disable Floppy Drive Seek

Floppy Drive Seek will force the BIOS to access the floppy drive during the boot sequence. This process can take several seconds, even with modern floppy drives.

If enabled, the Floppy Drive Seek BIOS option will attempt to detect and initialize the floppy drive during boot-up. If it cannot detect one, it will flash an error message. However, the system will still be allowed to continue the boot process. Whether it finds one or not, once Windows has loaded it becomes irrelevant anyway, as control of hardware devices, including drives, is handed over from the BIOS to the operating system.

Disable it as follows:

1 Enter the BIOS Setup program and open the Advanced BIOS Features page

2 Scroll down to Bootup Floppy Seek and select Disabled

Disabling Floppy Drive Seek will shave several seconds from the boot time on most systems.

Disable IDE Slot Auto-Detection

Every time a computer is booted, Windows checks all the IDE slots on the motherboard to see if a device is installed in them. This procedure, and hence the boot speed, can be speeded up by disabling auto-detection for any IDE slots that are not in use.

If you try the tip on this page, remember that you will need to re-enable auto-detection of the IDE slot should you subsequently decide to install a device in it.

1 Go to Start, Control Panel, System. Click the Hardware tab and then click Device Manager

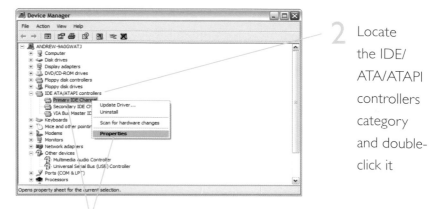

2 Locate the IDE/ ATA/ATAPI controllers category and double-click it

3 Right-click Primary IDE Channel, click Properties and then click the Advanced Settings tab

4 If either IDE slot on the controller is empty, the Device Type drop-down box will be active. Set it to None to disable auto-detection on that particular slot

5 Repeat the above steps for the Secondary IDE Channel

Shutdown Tweaks

Close Services Quickly

While XP is certainly no slouch, it does sometimes have a tendency to drag its heels when it comes to shutting down. There are several causes of this, one of which is that the system has to first close all running Services. Unfortunately, they don't always close as quickly as they should. To give them time to do so, XP is configured to wait a specified period before shutting down. The amount of time given is set in the Registry, and by modifying it, XP can be forced to shutdown more quickly. This is done as follows:

Technically, the tip on this page does not actually speed up shutdown. However, as it prevents XP's Services from delaying shutdown, the effect is the same.

1 Open the Registry Editor by typing regedit in the Run box

2 Find the following key:
   HKEY_LOCAL_MACHINE\System\CurrentControlSet\Control

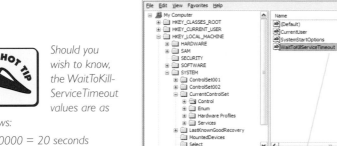

3 Click the Control folder

Should you wish to know, the WaitToKill-ServiceTimeout values are as follows:

- *20000 = 20 seconds*
- *10000 = 10 seconds*
- *5000 = 5 seconds*
- *1000 = 1 second*
- *500 = .5 seconds*
- *250 = .25 seconds*

4 Right-click WaitToKillServiceTimeout

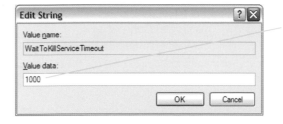

5 In the Value data box enter a lower number, such as 1000

Reboot XP, and you will now find that it shuts down much faster.

Automatically End Tasks on Shutdown

In the same way that a tardy Service can slow XP's shutdown routine, so can an application. In this situation XP will prompt the user for input. Until the user approves the closing of the program in question, the shutdown process will stop.

However, there is a registry setting that will make XP close non-responding applications automatically.

When an application fails to respond during shutdown, a dialog box is displayed prompting the user to either end it now or to wait. Enabling AutoEndTasks will close the non-responding application without user intervention. This is often referred to as "Force Exit".

Open the Registry Editor and locate the following key:
HKEY_CURRENT_USER\Control Panel\Desktop

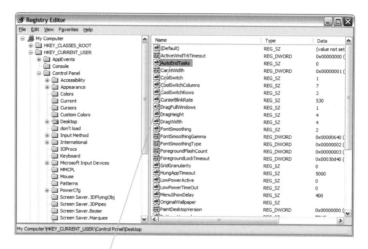

If you scroll down the window in step 1 opposite, you will see an entry called "HungAppTimeout." This setting determines the time it takes for Windows to invoke AutoEndTasks on non-responding applications. The default setting for this is 20000. Reducing it to 2000 will speed things up even more.

Double-click AutoEndTasks, and in the Value data box change the 0 to 1

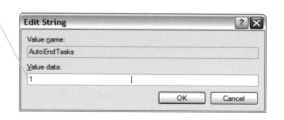

Reboot XP, and it will now be able to close non-responding applications without user input during the shutdown process, thus speeding it up.

System Customization

One of the most popular XP tips is how to avoid the need for logging on (going straight to the Desktop). Pages 50–51 show you how. We also offer a range of other tips relating to the changing of default system settings.

Covers

Chapter Three

Single-Click Operation

Something that many people are not aware of is that instead of clicking an item twice to open it, it can be done with a single-click. To enable this, do the following:

Single-click operation also saves you having to click an item in order to select it. When you place the cursor over an icon it will be automatically selected.

1 Open any folder, and from the menu bar select Tools and then Folder Options

2 Click the General tab

While you've got the Folder Options dialog box open, take a look at some of the other options available. For example, if you don't like the drop-down menus on the left-hand side of XP's folders, you can get rid of them by ticking Use Windows classic folders under Tasks.

3 Check "Single-click to open an item (point to select)" and click OK

From now on you can open any application with a single-click of the mouse.

Customize the Send To Menu

The Send To menu provides a very useful method of sending a file to an application not usually associated with that file type and simultaneously opening the file. You can also use it to save a file directly to a disk drive.

A typical example is opening a Notepad document in a word-processor. To do it, all you have to do is right-click the document, highlight Send To and click the application. It will then automatically open the document ready for use.

To illustrate how to add an item to the Send To menu, we will create a Send To option for a popular imaging program called Irfanview.

If you're curious, the Send To folder is located in the user's profile folder in Documents and Settings. It is, however, hidden by default. To access it, you will have to click the Tools menu in any open window, click Folder Options and then the View tab. Scroll down to "Show hidden files and folders" and tick it.

1 Right-click the program you want to add to the Send To menu (Irfanview in our example) and click Copy

2 Go to Start, Run and in the Run box, type sendto. This will open the Send To folder

3 Right-click in the Send To folder and then click Paste. This places the program's (Irfanview) shortcut into the folder

While the vast majority of programs work with XP's Send To feature, not all do. So if you try this and the program doesn't appear in the Send To menu, don't waste time trying to figure out why. Examples are programs from Microsoft Office Suites, such as Word, Excel and Frontpage.

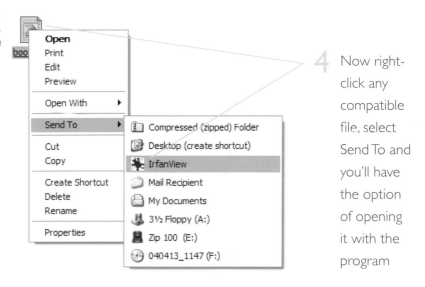

4 Now right-click any compatible file, select Send To and you'll have the option of opening it with the program

Speed Up XP's Start Menu

Many people find the default speed with which XP's Start menu opens to be on the slow side. This tip shows you how to make it open instantaneously.

Do the following:

It's your choice as to how fast you want the Start menu to open, but you may find that too low a setting will result in a menu that opens so quickly that it's almost unmanageable.

1 Open the Registry Editor and locate the following key: HKEY_CURRENT_USER\Control Panel\Desktop\ MenuShowDelay

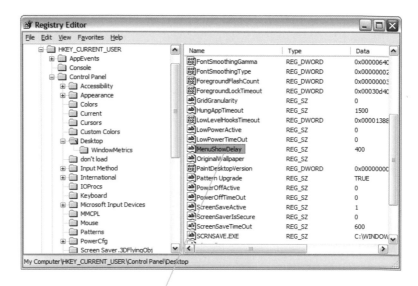

As with most Registry changes, you will need to reboot the computer before the changes made take effect.

2 Double-click MenuShowDelay to open its Edit box

3 Replace the default setting of 400 with a lower setting (100 in the example above). Experiment to find the one that suits you best

Rename the Recycle Bin

Given the opportunity, many people would call the Recycle Bin something else. Examples are Rubbish Bin, Garbage Can, etc. However, XP doesn't allow any options for doing this.

As it is a much requested tip, we'll show you how to do it, courtesy of a simple Registry tweak.

The Registry key required by this tip is quite difficult to find. If you can locate the key yourself, fine. However, you may find it easier to do it as described on this page.

1. Go to Start, All Programs, Accessories, Notepad. In Notepad, type the following, exactly as it is written:

Windows Registry Editor Version 5.00

[HKEY_CLASSES_ROOT\CLSID\{645FF040-5081-101B-9F08-00AA002F954E}\ShellFolder]

"Attributes"=hex:50,01,00,20

"CallForAttributes"=dword:00000000

Save time when deleting files by disabling the "Delete Confirmation" dialog box that pops up every time you delete a file. Do this by right-clicking the Recycle Bin and removing the check from the relevant box.

2. Give this file a name (any name will do), give it a Registry file extension, i.e. aaa.reg and then save it to the Desktop. Click the icon that appears and you will see the following dialog box:

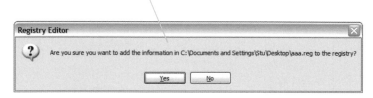

If you are quite certain that a file will not be needed again, press the Shift key as you delete it. Doing this will bypass the Recycle Bin completely.

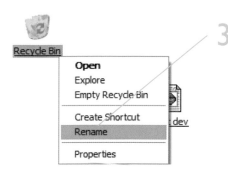

3. Click Yes and then reboot for the change to take effect. From now on, right-clicking the Recycle Bin will reveal an option called Rename. Click this and you will be able to call it what you like

How to Change File Associations

All files are designed to be opened with a specific type of program. For example, graphics files such as JPEG and GIF can only be opened by a graphics editing program, e.g. Photoshop, or with a Web browser such as Internet Explorer.

A common problem that many users experience is when they install a program on their PC that makes itself the default program for opening related files. A good example of this is some versions of Paint Shop Pro.

If the user prefers the original program, he or she will have to reassociate the file type in question. Alternatively, the user might want to make a different program the default one.

This is done as follows:

1 Open any folder and from the Tools menu select Folder Options

The File Types dialog box lists every registered file type on the computer. In most circumstances, the user will not need to make any changes here. However, should the need arise, it is worth knowing how to reassociate file types.

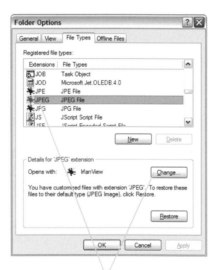 

2 Select the file type whose association you want to change and click Change

3 In the Open With dialog box, select the program you want to open the file type with. Then click OK

Mouse Snap-To

This tip will eliminate the need to move your mouse to a certain extent, by making the cursor jump automatically to the default button whenever a new dialog box is opened.
Set this up as follows:

Enabling the Mouse Snap-To feature is particularly useful if you are in the habit of using the keyboard. By having the cursor move automatically to the default button in a dialog box, it is easier to see which button or option has focus and will be activated when you press ENTER.

1   Go to Start, Control Panel, Mouse

2   Click the Pointer Options tab

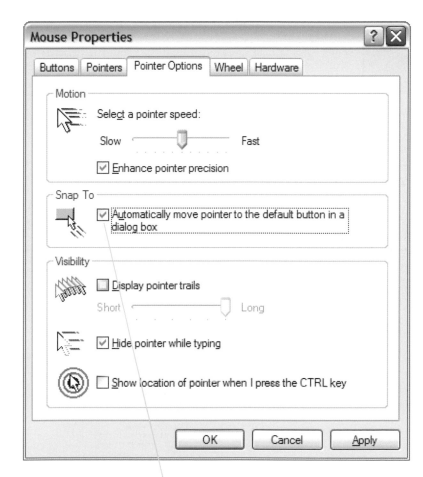

In the same dialog box, you can increase the speed at which the cursor moves by dragging the slider under "Select a pointer speed" to "Fast."

3   Click here to put a check in this box

Try it out. Some people hate it, others love it.

Customize XP's Thumbnail Sizes

In any folder, when you click the View button on the menu bar, you are presented with a Thumbnail option. When selected, Windows will display all the files in that folder as thumbnails (miniature pictures). If the file is a graphic then that graphic will be displayed instead of the file's original icon.

This feature can be extremely useful in certain applications – a photo album for example. The drawback is that when you open a folder in this mode, the thumbnails will appear very slowly. Also, if the folder contains many files, you will have to do a lot of scrolling to see them all.

By changing this setting under HKEY_ LOCAL_ MACHINE, you are altering the thumbnail size for all users of the computer (assuming you have the PC setup for more than one user).

To restrict the setting to the current user (the user changing the setting), follow the same procedure, only do it under:

HKEY_CURRENT_USER\ Software\Microsoft\Windows\ CurrentVersion\Explorer.

The default size of XP's thumbnails is quite large, which exacerbates this problem. However, there is a way to reduce them, and this is as follows:

1   Open the Registry Editor by typing regedit in the Run box

2   Locate the following registry key:
HKEY_LOCAL_MACHINE\Software\Microsoft\Windows\
CurrentVersion\Explorer

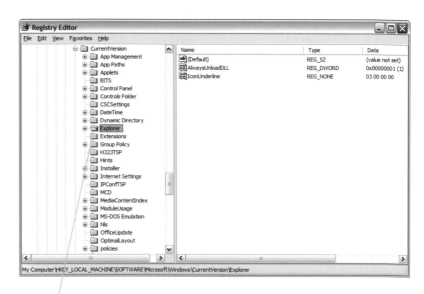

3   Click the Explorer folder

4 On the right-hand side of the window, right-click and select New DWORD Value. You will see a new entry – New Value #1. Rename this to Thumbnailsize

By clicking Views on the menu bar of any window and selecting Thumbnails, the icon of any graphic files in that folder will become a small representation of the graphic. This also applies to video files; in this case you will see a graphic of the opening scene.

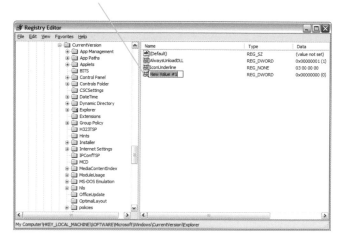

5 Right-click Thumbnailsize and then click Modify

6 Type 32 in the Value data box. Click OK, close the Registry Editor and reboot the PC

Should you wish to disable XP's Thumbnail view option for some reason, do the following:

Locate the registry key at:

HKEY_CURRENT_USER\ Software\Microsoft\Windows\ CurrentVersion\Explorer\ Advanced

In the right-hand window, double-click ClassicViewState and change its Data value to 1.

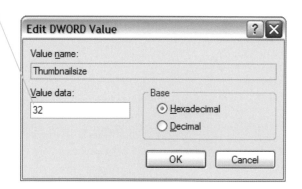

Your thumbnails will now be considerably smaller than before. 32 will give you the minimum size while 256 gives the maximum. Experiment to find the size that suits you best.

Hide Frequently Used Programs List

A feature new to XP's Start Menu places the most frequently accessed applications on the lower left-hand side of the menu. This list updates automatically according to the frequency with which individual programs are run. It would appear, however, that this is not one of XP's most popular features, and that many people would do away with it if they could.

This is, in fact, very simple to do.

Another way is to simply revert to the classic Windows Start menu. Click Start, right-click on the top or bottom of the menu and select Properties. Click the Start Menu tab and then tick Classic Start menu.

1 Right-click at the top or bottom of the Start menu and select Properties. This opens the Taskbar and Start Menu Properties dialog box

2 Click Start menu and then click Customize

3 Click the Clear List button

You can also specify how many programs are displayed in the Frequently Used Programs list by setting a number in the "Number of programs on Start menu" box. This ranges from 0 to 30. Using the 0 setting has the same effect as pressing the Clear List button.

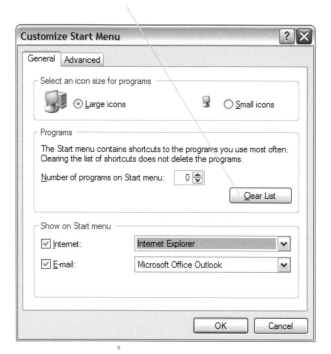

Now go back to the Start menu and the Frequently Used Programs list will have disappeared.

However, if you find this feature useful and just want to prevent certain programs from being displayed, you can do a selective block as follows:

You can remove a specific program from the Frequently Used Programs list by right-clicking and clicking Remove from this list. However, this does not prevent the program reappearing if you continue to use it. The tip on this page will block it permanently.

1 Open the Registry Editor as previously described and locate the following key:

HKEY_CLASSES_ROOT\Applications\Program name.exe

("Program name.exe" is the program you want to block)

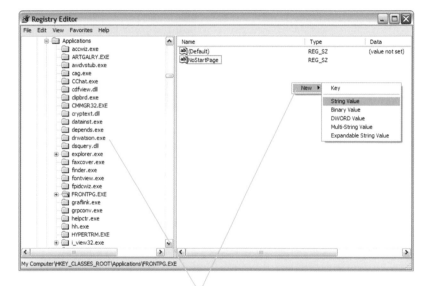

2 Click the program's folder and in the right-hand window, right-click to create a new String value. Double-click this and name it NoStartPage

3 Close the Registry Editor and reboot the PC for the change to take effect

The application in question will now never be displayed on the Frequently Used Programs list – very handy for hiding from the boss the fact that you play FreeCell all day.

Log on Automatically to XP

With a single-user account setup, when booted, XP goes directly to the Desktop. However, as soon as another user account is added, boot-up stops at the Welcome screen, as shown below:

Another method of enabling auto-logon is to install a program called TweakUI (see page 180). This is available from the Microsoft website and when installed it can be accessed from the All Programs menu. Open TweakUI and click Autologon. Check the box titled Log on automatically at system startup, enter your user-name and password, and click OK.

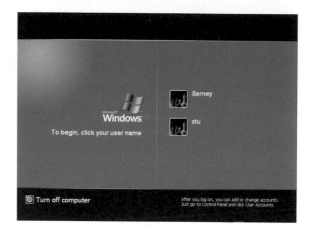

To continue booting, the desired account must be selected. Many people won't want this; they'd rather go straight to the Desktop. The way to do it is as follows:

1 Go to Start, Control Panel, User Accounts. Click Change the way users log on or off

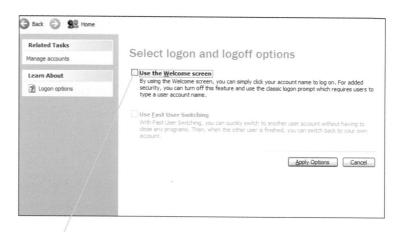

2 Uncheck Use the Welcome screen.

Enabling automatic logon will prevent other users from accessing their accounts when the computer is booted. This can be resolved by holding down the Shift key as soon as XP's splash screen appears. This overrides auto-logon and brings up the Welcome screen from where all the PC's accounts can be accessed.

However, doing this will simply replace the Welcome screen with the logon box shown opposite, so you are no better off – you still have to click your way into Windows.

Get rid of the logon box as follows:

1 Go to Start, Run. In the Run box, type control userpasswords2

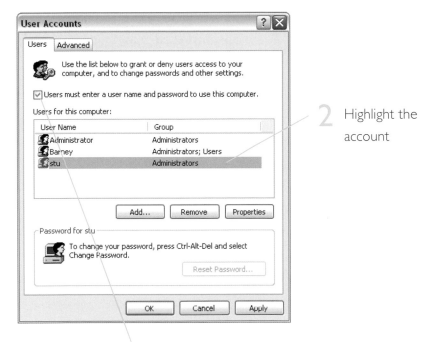

2 Highlight the account

3 Remove the check mark from the "Users must enter a user name and password to use this computer" box

Reboot, and this time the computer will boot directly to the Windows Desktop.

Remove Shared Documents Folders

When you open My Computer, right at the top, you will see a Shared Folder, plus a Documents folder for each user. According to Microsoft, they: "provide a place for you to store files, pictures, and music that everyone on your computer can access." However, judging by popular reaction, this is a feature that not too many people actually want. Get rid of the shared folders as described below:

Unlike personal folders, shared folders cannot be made private as described on page 92. The contents of these folders are always available to anyone who uses the computer. The only way to prevent this is to disable the folders completely as described opposite.

Open the Registry Editor and locate the following key: HKEY_LOCAL_MACHINE\Software\Microsoft\Windows\CurrentVersion\Explorer\My Computer\NameSpace\DelegateFolders

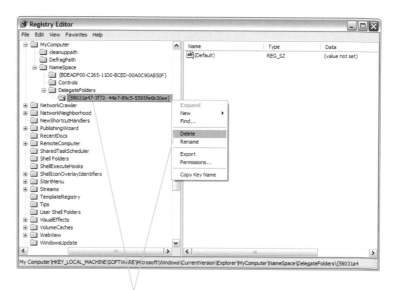

2   Click the + sign next to DelegateFolder and delete the subkey. Close the Registry and the Shared Documents folders will be gone

XP Annoyances

Good operating system though it undoubtedly is, XP does have some quirks that many people find irritating.

This chapter shows how to eliminate the most common of these.

Covers

Chapter Four

Say Goodbye to Error Reports

Whenever an application suffers from an error and is closed down by the system, the Microsoft Error Reporting feature will pop up, asking if you want to send a report about the problem to Microsoft.

Windows Error Reporting (WER), sends detailed reports when programs crash. These are used to alert manufacturers to bugs in their software, thus enabling them to either fix the problems, or to offer patches or work-arounds.

Programs must be specially written to use WER. Microsoft uses WER in all recent programs and strongly encourages other companies to do the same.

It all relies, however, on the user sending the report in the first place.

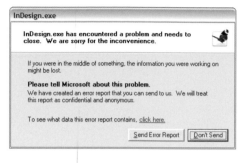

If you're the one in a million who will actually comply, then read no further. However, if you've no intention of ever doing it, then you'll want to get rid of this irritation as soon as possible.

You can do it as follows:

Go to Start, Control Panel, System. Select the Advanced tab

The error reporting dialog box shown opposite, allows the user to be selective about which programs will be reported. Clicking Choose Programs will open a new dialog box in which you can specify any programs you do not want to be reported.

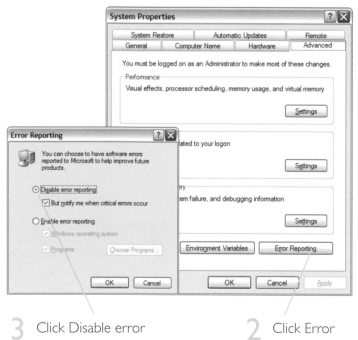

3 Click Disable error reporting and click OK

2 Click Error Reporting

Banish New Program Messages

Apart from throwing up a pop-up message as shown opposite, the Highlight newly installed programs feature also highlights the program in the All Programs menu as shown below.

The tip on this page will also remove this highlighting.

This message has an irritating habit of popping up just as you are trying to access the All Programs, Log Off or Turn off Computer buttons, and can be extremely annoying as it gets in the way.

Fortunately, there is a way to prevent it:

1   Open the Start menu and right-click at the top or bottom. Then select Properties

2   This opens the Taskbar and Start Menu Properties dialog box. On the Start menu tab click Customize, and then in the Customize Start Menu dialog box, click the Advanced tab

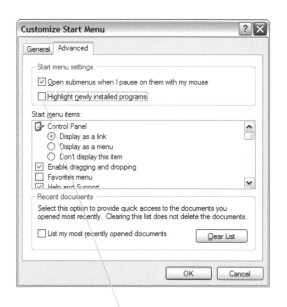

3   Now remove the check mark from the Highlight newly installed programs box

Hide the Logon Email Message Alert

When XP is started, it will indicate at the Welcome screen if any users have unread emails in their Inbox. For any number of reasons, people might not wish other users of the computer to know this. Turn the feature off as follows:

The unread email message counter that appears on the XP Welcome screen can sometimes indicate that more unread messages exist than is actually the case. There are several causes of this; a common one being when another user accesses the machine to check his or her email while you're logged on.

1 Open the Registry Editor and locate the following key: HKEY_CURRENT_USER\Software\Microsoft\Windows\Current Version\Unreadmail

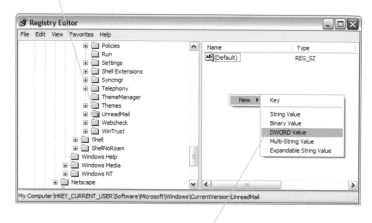

2 Right-click in the right-hand window and create a new DWORD Value. Name it MessageExpiryDays

TweakUI (see page 180) has a setting that will perform the tweak on this page for you automatically.

3 Right-click the new entry, choose Modify, and in the Edit DWORD Value dialog box, enter a Value data of 0

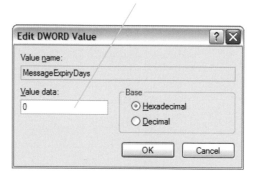

4 Restart the PC for the change to take effect

Puncture Those Balloon Tips

XP has an irritating habit of throwing up balloon tips that give the user various types of information. Much of it is obvious or will already be known.

While most of the information imparted by balloon tips is obvious to the user, or nagging, occasionally they will come up with something worth knowing. For example, if your system is running low on memory, you will get a balloon tip warning you of the fact. Disable them at your own risk.

For those of you who can do without these tips, the solution is as follows:

1   Fire-up the Registry Editor and locate the following key:
    HKEY_CURRENT_USER\Software\Microsoft\
    Windows\CurrentVersion\Explorer\Advanced

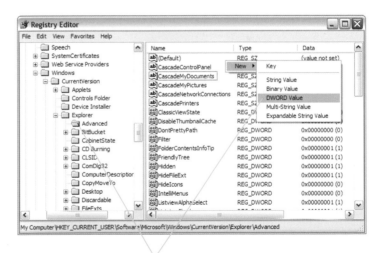

2   Click the Advanced folder and on the right-hand side, right-click and select New DWORD Value. Name it EnableBalloonTips

3   Double-click this and enter 0 in the Value data box

Reboot and from now on you will never see another balloon tip.

Cancel Unsigned Driver Warnings

Whether or not you take heed of unsigned driver warnings is entirely up to you. In the vast majority of cases, the driver concerned will be perfectly good. However, if you install a bad one, you could be introducing system instability and other related problems to your PC. The only way to be absolutely certain that a driver is suitable for XP is when it doesn't invoke the warning message. If it does, visit the manufacturer's website where you might well find an updated driver that has been certified for use with XP.

Incompatible device drivers can render an XP system extremely unstable and be the cause of crashes and lock-ups. To try and prevent this, all drivers designed for use with XP will, ideally, be approved by Microsoft and given an electronic "signature." Any driver that doesn't have this signature will, when installed, invoke XP's unsigned driver warning message, as shown above.

You can stop these messages appearing by doing the following:

1 Go to Start, Control Panel, System. Click the Hardware tab and then click Driver Signing

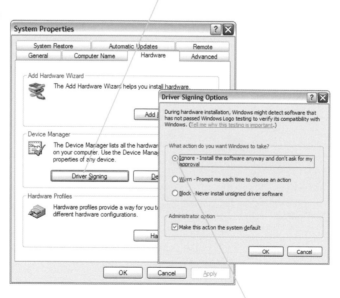

2 Select "Ignore – install the software anyway and don't ask for my approval"

Set the Correct Refresh Rate

The author recently repaired a friends PC, and while doing so reset the refresh rate to 85 (it was previously set to 60). This was causing the display to flicker rapidly. On getting the PC back, the first thing the friend noticed was how much more stable the picture was.

This highlights an issue that is specific to XP; namely, the fact that when installed, it always sets the refresh rate to a less than optimal level. The result is extremely irritating flickering of the display.

If you haven't already done so, check this out.

Right-click the Desktop, select Properties, click the Settings tab and then Advanced

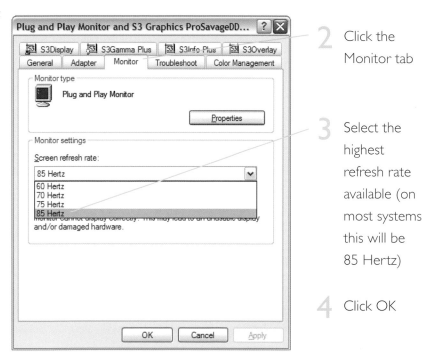

2 Click the Monitor tab

3 Select the highest refresh rate available (on most systems this will be 85 Hertz)

4 Click OK

The screen will now go blank for a few seconds before reappearing with a dialog box asking if you want to keep the new setting. Click Yes to accept the new refresh rate. You will now have a flicker-free display that will be much kinder on your eyes.

Shoot the Messenger

Don't confuse Windows Messenger with XP's Messenger Service (see page 143). They are completely different applications.

Windows Messenger is a communication program that can be used for file transfer, messages, video conferencing, etc.

The program loads automatically with Windows and sits in the system tray (notification area) where it is ready for use. Many people do indeed use it and find it extremely useful. Many others, however, never use it and find the fact that it's always there and that there's no apparent way of removing it, somewhat irritating.

If all you want to do is prevent Messenger from running, do the following:

The screenshots on this page were taken from the latest version of Windows Messenger – version 6.2. If you are running an earlier version, in step 1, you will need to click the Preferences tab rather than the General tab.

1 Open Windows Messenger, and from the Tools tab, click Options. Click the General tab

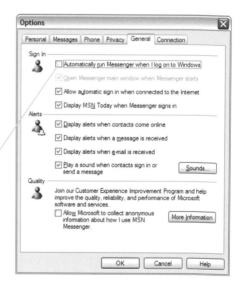

Should you ever wish to get Windows Messenger back, you can download the latest version from Microsoft's website. This is a small 5 MB file.

2 Untick the "Automatically run Messenger when I log on to Windows" box

If you'd rather get rid of it completely, however, go to Start, Run. In the Run box, type the following (including spaces):

RunDll32 advpack.dll,LaunchINFSection %windir%\INF\msmsgs. inf,BLC.Remove

Press OK to uninstall Windows Messenger.

Cosmetic Customization

Windows XP is a "tweakers" paradise, allowing all manner of changes to its default settings. This chapter shows just a few of the ways you can change the way XP looks.

Covers

Chapter Five

Restore Familiar Desktop Icons

On running XP for the first time many people are surprised to see that with the exception of the Recycle Bin, all the usual Desktop icons have disappeared. Get them back as follows:

1 Right-click the Desktop and select Properties

Using the tip on this page will only enable you to add My Computer, My Network Places, My Documents and Internet Explorer to the Desktop. However, you can add the icons of most other applications simply by right-clicking and selecting Send To, Desktop (create shortcut).

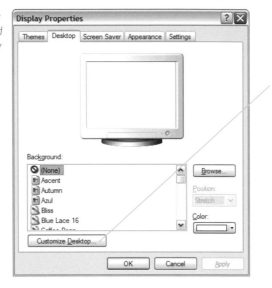

2 Click the Desktop tab and then click Customize Desktop

You can also use this dialog box to change the default icons. You aren't given a great deal of choice though, so if nothing appeals, take a look at page 69, which shows you how to access a greater range of icons.

3 Check the boxes next to the items you want to restore

4 Click OK

How to Configure XP's Taskbar

Another thing that will be immediately noticeable on running XP for the first time is that the Quick Launch toolbar has disappeared from the Taskbar. This is just one of several changes to the traditional Windows Taskbar.

To get the Quick Launch toolbar back, simply right-click on an empty part of the Taskbar and you will see a pop-up menu:

As with previous versions of Windows, you can resize the Taskbar or move it to any edge of the screen. If it won't move, right-click an empty area and uncheck "Lock Taskbar."

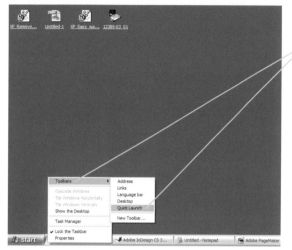

Select Toolbars and then click Quick Launch

A new Taskbar feature is the grouping of related applications. Say, for example, that you have three different Notepad documents open at the same time. On the Taskbar you will see "3 Notepad." Click it and you will get a pop-up window showing you the names of the three documents. You can then easily maximize or close them, either individually or collectively. The purpose of this feature is to keep the Taskbar free of clutter.

The Links and Desktop toolbars can be restored in the same way as the Quick Launch. Whereas in previous Windows versions, the various items would be spread out along the Taskbar, in XP, you get a single entry which opens a pop-up menu showing every item on the toolbar. These menus can be expanded further to show all links and sub-links to these items.

2 Clicking Desktop reveals a pop-up menu leading to sub-menus

Lose XP's New Look

The most obvious change from previous versions of Windows is the appearance of the Windows XP interface. Gone is the somewhat conservative look, and in its place is what some would describe as a scheme bordering on the garish, with chunky and brightly colored buttons.

Needless to say, many people are not all that keen on it. It would seem that Microsoft anticipated this reaction, and so have provided a way to restore the familiar look of Windows.

The Windows Classic theme removes the XP components from Windows and thus makes it resemble the older versions – to a certain extent. The familiar icons will still be missing from the Desktop, the Start menu won't be the same and folders will have a shortcut taskbar on the left. However, if you are determined enough to find them, there are enough tweaks available to enable you to more or less recreate the old Windows look. For example, you can make folders look like they used to by clicking Tools on the menu bar, clicking Folder Options, and selecting Use Windows classic folders.

1 Right-click the Desktop and click Properties. Then click the Themes tab

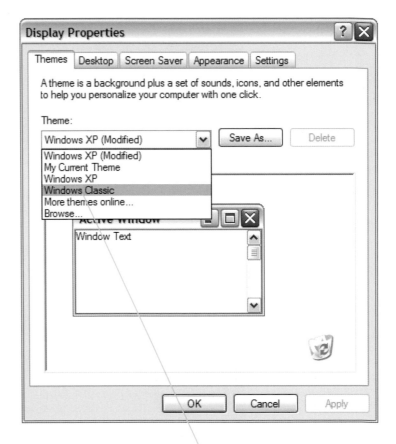

2 Using the drop-down box, select Windows Classic and then click OK. The old Windows look will be restored

Change XP's Icons

This tip will work with Windows applications such as Internet Explorer and Outlook Express. You can also try it with third-party programs you have installed yourself. Most of them will give you a choice of icons.

As with its interface scheme, XP comes with a set of new-look icons. Again, these aren't to everybody's taste and fortunately it's an easy task to change them to something more to your liking.

To change the icon of a system folder such as My Computer or Neighborhood Network, you first have to create a shortcut to the folder. To demonstrate this we will change the icon for My Computer.

1   Right-click the My Computer icon and click Create Shortcut

2   Right-click the shortcut, click Properties and then Change Icon. This will open an icon folder. Make a selection and then click OK

If you can't find an icon that appeals, you will find literally thousands on the Internet. All you have to do is search them out and download them. It is a good idea to create a specific folder for this purpose. To associate downloaded icons with a particular application, in step 2 opposite, use the Browse button to find your icon folder. Open it, select the icon and then click OK.

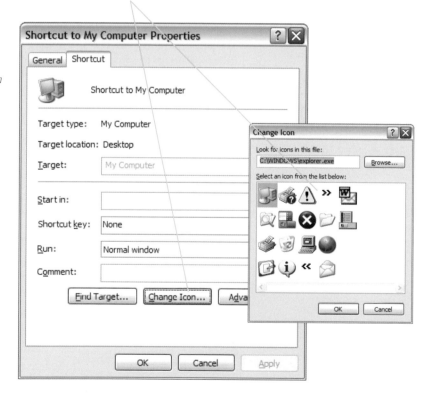

The list of icons obtained by the tip opposite is very small. See page 69 for how to access a much greater range of icons.

3   Now all you need to do is delete the original My Computer icon. This procedure will work for most system folders. You will also find that most applications will give you several choices of icon

How to Customize Folder Icons

Quite apart from changing icons for system folders and stand-alone applications, XP allows you to change, and also customize, individual folder icons. This is something that required a third-party utility in previous versions of Windows.

Putting pictures on icons might seem silly to some people, but it can actually be a very useful method of identifying a folder's contents. For example, you could create text graphics to place on your folders. These could read, Stu's Photo's, Stu's Letters, Stu's Accounts or anything else you want.

Right-click the folder you want to customize and then click Properties. In the dialog box select the Customize tab

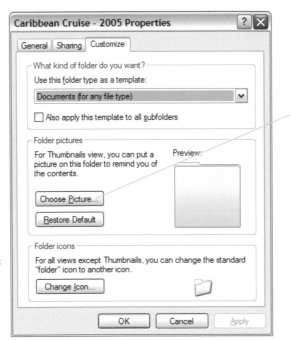

The only drawback with the tip on this page is the fact that the folder will only display the picture if Thumbnail is selected under Views on the folder's menu bar. This means that a folder's picture will not be displayed if it is placed on the Desktop as there are no View options for Desktop items.

2 To customize the folder by placing a picture on it, click Choose Picture. Browse to your desired picture and double-click it

3 The picture will be placed on the folder icon

Caribbean Cruise - 2005

Using pictures is a useful and fun way of personalizing folders, and also provides a useful method of identifying their contents.

By clicking the Change Icon button in the folders Properties dialog box, you can also select a different icon for the folder.

Create Your Own Icons

XP comes with a good supply of icons and most people are perfectly happy to use these. However, it is quite a simple task to create and use your own.

You can either design the icon yourself using an image editing program such as Windows Paint, or simply convert any image to an icon.

Design Your Icon Using Paint

Open Paint by going to Start, All Programs, Accessories, Paint. Click Image on the toolbar and select Attributes.

In the Width and Height boxes, overwrite the current values by typing 32 in each (this is the standard icon size)

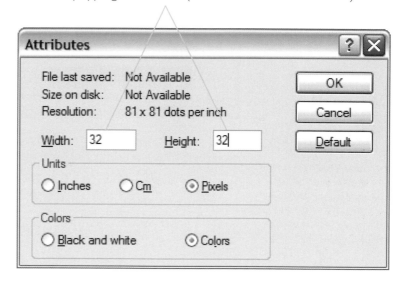

2   You'll notice that the workspace has now shrunk. Increase it by going to View on the menu bar and then Zoom, and Custom. Select the 800% setting

3   Click View, Zoom, and Show Grid. This will grid the workspace making it easier to create your icon accurately. Also, click Show Thumbnail. This will enable you to see how your icon looks as you are creating it

始：

4 Create your icon using Paint's drawing tools

When you have created your new icon, you must save it as a bitmap. Also, you must "make" it an icon by giving it the icon file extension ".ico" placed immediately after the name.

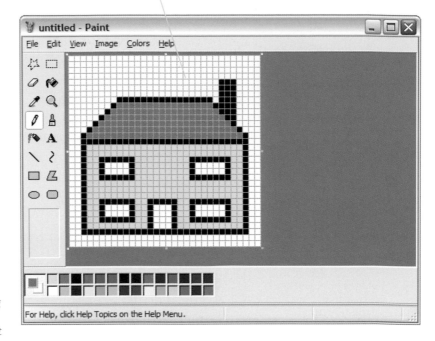

Using an existing image to create an icon will result in a file size of anything up to 1MB. Creating it yourself with an image editing program will result in a file size of roughly 5KB – quite a difference. There is a way around this, but to do it you will need a more powerful program than Paint. A good choice would be Paint Shop Pro. This program has features that will enable you to reduce the file size of an icon created from an image file.

5 When your icon is finished, you need to save it as an icon file. This is done by using the .ico file extension. Click Save As from the File menu, give your icon a name, e.g. House.ico and save it in a folder. It's a good idea to create an icon folder for this purpose

Creating an icon from an existing image is even easier. Simply open the image in Paint, give it a suitable name followed by the .ico file extension, and then save it as a bitmap to your icon folder.

To apply your new icons use the method described on page 65. The only difference is that you must browse to the folder containing your icons and select them from there.

Uncover XP's Hidden Icons

The tip on this page (and the one on page 65) allows you to only associate a system icon with the program shortcut used to view the contents of the icon folder. If you want to do more than this (move or copy the icons to a different folder, etc), you will need a program capable of accessing an icon .dll file. There are many of these freely available on the Internet.

Windows XP comes with hundreds of icons which are hidden away in files with the .dll extension. The three main icon files can be located as described below:

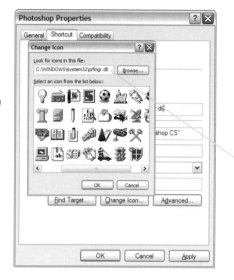

1 Right-click any shortcut, click Properties and then Change Icon

2 In the box, type: C:\WINDOWS\system32\pifmgr.dll. Press OK to open the icon file

3 Another icon file can be accessed by typing: C:\WINDOWS\system32\shell32.dll

4 Yet another icon file can be opened by typing: C:\WINDOWS\system32\moricons.dll

Get Rid of Shortcut Arrows

All shortcuts are identified by a little arrow pointing upwards to the icon and many people don't like them. Fortunately, there is a way to get rid of them.

Having removed the shortcut arrows you might also like to get rid of the prefix "Shortcut to..." which precedes all shortcuts. Doing this will make your shortcuts appear as normal icons. All you have to do is right-click the shortcut and then rename it, e.g. "Shortcut to Drive C" could be renamed "Drive C".

1 Open the Registry Editor, click Edit and then Find

2 Type: IsShortcut then click Find Next

IsShortcut is the Registry entry which refers to the shortcut arrows. We have to find all instances and delete them. When the Registry finds an instance you will see the following:

You will find that there are six instances of IsShortcut in XP Home Edition. Keep pressing the F3 key and deleting until they are all gone.

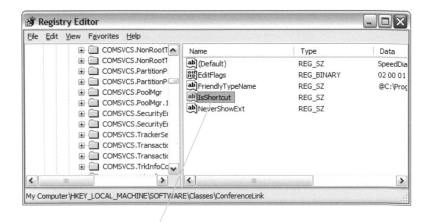

3 Delete IsShortcut by right-clicking and clicking Delete. Hit the F3 keyboard key to repeat the search. Delete the next instance of IsShortcut, and repeat this procedure until all instances have been removed. Reboot, and all those pesky arrows will be gone for good.

Create Your Own Wallpaper

XP comes with a reasonably good selection of wallpaper which is stored in the Windows folder. You select them from the Desktop tab in the Display Properties dialog box.

As has already been pointed out on page 33, having your Desktop elaborately wallpapered will increase the computer's boot-up time.

However, should you find these uninspiring, it's a simple matter to create your own. All you need is the raw material and XP's graphic editor, Paint (Start, All Programs, Accessories, Paint).

The first thing to do is to open your graphic in Paint. This can be a photo you have scanned-in to the PC or something you have designed yourself.

Do what editing is necessary, then give it the correct dimensions. You can ascertain what these are by right-clicking the Desktop, clicking Properties and then clicking the Settings tab. At the lower left-hand side you will see the screen resolution to which your monitor is set (800 x 600, 1024 x 768, etc.). This is what you need to know. Go back to Paint and click Image, Attributes. This opens the Attributes dialog box.

If you don't like any of XP's wallpapers and you can't be bothered to make your own, the Internet is where you need to go. Here you will find a vast assortment freely available for download.

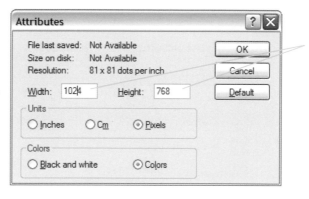

Enter the dimensions in the Width and Height boxes and click OK

Now go to File, Save As. Give your wallpaper a name and then, in the Save as Type box, select 24-bit Bitmap. Finally, in the Save In box, browse to the Windows folder. Open the folder and then click Save.

The next time you go to the Desktop tab in Display Properties, your wallpaper will be there along with the default wallpapers.

Create a Personal Screensaver

This is a simple tip that is very easy to do. All you need is a supply of pictures. Scanned-in photos from a photo album would be ideal. To create the screensaver do the following:

Right-click the Desktop and select Properties. This opens the Display Properties dialog box. Click the Screensaver tab

2 Using the drop-down box, click My Pictures Slideshow and then click Settings

In the My Pictures Screen Saver Options dialog box, you can also configure the way your screensaver runs. For example, you can set the time delay between pictures, the size of the displayed picture, and add transition effects.

3 In the My Pictures Screen Saver Options dialog box, click Browse. Locate the folder containing your pictures, highlight it and then click OK

Change User Picture Icons

For anyone who may be interested, the exact location of XP's user pictures folder is C:\Documents and Settings\All Users\Application Data\Microsoft\User Account Pictures.

Note that the Application Data folder is hidden by default. To "unhide" it, open any folder and click Tools. Then click Folder Options, click the View tab, and finally, click Show hidden files and folders.

Each time an account is created, XP assigns it a user picture to help identify the account, and also add a bit of visual interest. Many people use picture icons to personalize their account. These pictures will be seen to the left of the account name on the logon screen and at the top-left of the Start menu.

XP supplies 23 of these, and the default picture is one of a guitar. However, it's quite simple to make your own choice as described below:

1 Go to Start, Control Panel, User Accounts. Click the relevant account

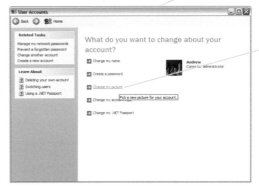

2 In the User Accounts dialog box, click Change my picture

Not everybody will find XP's list of user pictures to their taste. Many will prefer to use one of their own. You can do this as follows:

1) Having got your picture, use a graphics program to resize it to 48 x 48 pixels

2) Save the picture in the My Pictures folder (see margin note above)

3) Follow steps 1 and 2 on this page to open XP's user picture folder, as shown opposite

4) Click Browse for more pictures and the My Pictures folder will open. Select the picture you want

3 Choose the picture you want and then click Change Picture

Change the Logon Bitmap

XP's logon bitmap is a plain blue screen that is displayed for a few seconds before the Welcome screen appears. For those of you who like to customize everything in sight, this can be changed to whatever you want – a photograph of the user, for example. Do it as follows:

For this tip to work you must enter the full path of the bitmap, plus its name. If you aren't sure about this simply right-click the bitmap file and then click Properties. Next to Location you will see the full path of the file. Highlight this with your mouse, right-click it and select Copy. Then in the Value data box (Step 3) just click Paste. You will then need to follow this with a backslash and the name of the file.

1 Open the Registry Editor by typing regedit in the Run box, available from the Start menu

2 Locate the following registry key: HKEY_USERS\.DEFAULT\Control Panel\Desktop

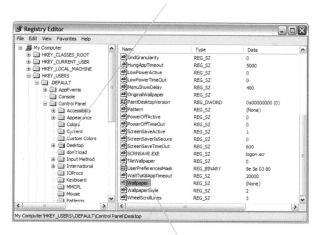

3 In the right-hand window, scroll down to the entry called Wallpaper, right-click it and click Modify. In the Value data box, enter the full path and name of the bitmap you wish to use

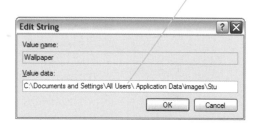

4 Restart XP and your chosen bitmap will now flash up for a few seconds before the Welcome screen appears

Add Extra Themes to XP

Earlier Windows versions have been somewhat conservative in their default interface look. XP though, takes a more imaginative approach with its bright and colorful appearance.

Unfortunately, it only comes with three themes: the default Blue, Olive Green and Silver, so the user isn't given much choice.

However, by firing up your browser and heading off into cyber-space, you will discover that there is a virtually limitless amount of themes, or "Skins" as they are often called, available for download.

These come in an infinite range of colors and styles, and will enable you to radically change the way XP looks.

The illustrations below show just two examples:

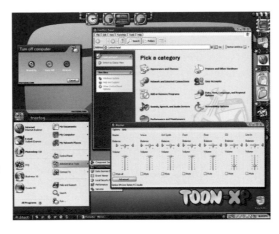

Themes come with customized Windows, icons, wallpaper, and sometimes with related sound effects as well

All themes downloaded from the Internet require the use of a third-party program such as "Window Blinds"

How to Display a Logon Message

Should you ever wish to alter or remove the message, simply repeat steps 1 to 3, this time amending or deleting the caption and message.

In certain situations, it can be useful to greet users of a computer with a message when they logon. This might simply be something friendly and welcoming, or a warning of some description. An example of the latter could occur in an office environment where it is common for company email and Internet facilities to be misused.

1 Open the Registry Editor and locate the following key: HKEY_LOCAL_MACHINE\Software\Microsoft\WindowsNT\ CurrentVersion\Winlogon

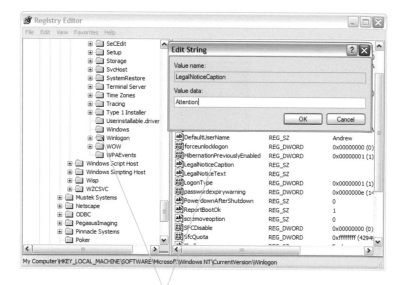

2 Click the Winlogon folder, and in the right-hand window double-click LegalNoticeCaption. In the Value data box, type your caption, e.g. Attention

3 Repeat steps 1 and 2 with LegalNoticeText. In the Value data box, type the message you want to be displayed

Reboot the computer and your captioned message will be displayed before the logon screen.

Multimedia

Gaming is one of the most popular applications to which a PC is put. However, as PCs are not designed specifically for game playing (as are PlayStations and X-Boxes), the results are often less than satisfactory. This chapter gives some tips on how to maximize the performance of your games.

You will also find some handy hints regarding multimedia in general.

Covers

Chapter Six

Get Media Player 2 Back

The media player bundled with XP is a radical departure from the classic Media Player 2 that was a stalwart of older versions of

If, for some reason, you want the look of Media Player 2 while retaining all the features of the new player, you can apply a Media Player 2 "skin" from the skin-chooser toolbar.

There are also many other skins from which to choose.

Windows. It has a much busier interface, and a whole range of new features, such as CD burning capabilities. For all that, however, it still doesn't play movies any better than Media Player 2 does.

While Media Player 2 is still

Media Player 2 is actually located in the Windows Media Player folder in the Programs folder.

available with XP, Microsoft have seen fit to hide it away. Also, all the movie file formats are associated with the new player.

You can get it back as follows:

1. In the Start menu Run box, type mplayer2 and click OK. Make it the default player as described in steps 2 and 3 below

2. From the menu bar, select View and then Options. Click the Formats tab

3. Choose the file formats you want to open with Media Player 2 by ticking the check boxes. This will make it the default player for these file types

Keep the CDs in the Drawer

One of the most irritating things about playing games is the constant need for inserting and changing CDs. Apart from being a nuisance, a well-used CD can eventually become scratched enough to prevent it playing properly.

Many people try copying the CD to the hard drive and then installing the game from there. This will work, but only up to the point where you try to run the game – then you will get a "No disk in CD drive" error message. This is manufacturers' copy protection at work.

However, there is a way to eliminate CD-changing. To do it, you need a virtual CD-ROM drive. This is an emulated drive created by a software program. The software creates an image of the game CD on the hard drive, which can then be played in the virtual drive; the real CD is not required at all. A good example of this type of program is "CDSpace" (shown below), available from www.cdspace.com.

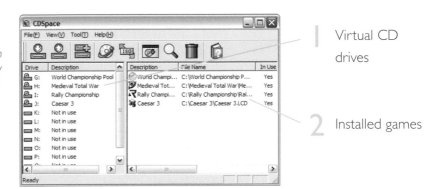

Virtual CD drives

Installed games

Virtual CD-ROM programs can create up to 23 virtual CD drives, which means you can have up to 23 different games pre-loaded and ready to go. You can put the CDs in a drawer and forget about them.

Also, as the games are being played from the hard drive, they will perform better.

Use the Correct Graphic Format

If you do a lot of image editing, a good imaging program is well worth buying. Apart from the usual brightness and contrast adjustments, they will also allow you to remove blemishes, lighten shadows, correct over- and under-exposure, and remove background objects.

The best one is Photoshop but this is, unfortunately, extremely expensive. Photoshop Elements, Paint Shop Pro and Microsoft's Picture It are good alternatives.

Graphics (images or video), use a variety of formats, each of which are suitable for specific purposes. This section will show you which type to use, and when.

Images

One of the most popular uses of PCs is the storage and editing of digital images. These can be images downloaded from the Internet, scanned-in with a scanner or taken with a digital camera. Imaging programs such as Photoshop allow the user to touch-up the images (brightening, cropping, red-eye removal, etc.). When the editing is complete, the file then has to be saved, and it's at this point that mistakes are often made. All good imaging programs will offer you a large choice of file formats in which to save your images. The question is, which?

The ones you need to consider are explained below:

GIF – this is a low-size image format, which is mostly found on websites where it is used for small low-quality images such as advertising banners, clip art, etc. GIF only supports 256 colors or shades of gray: this makes it unsuitable for professional imaging. Only save a file to this format if you want the lowest possible file size and the quality of the image is not important.

TIFF files can be enormous in size. This makes them impractical for storing large amounts of image files. You will only need to use this format when the image concerned is to be printed at a high resolution.

BITMAP – Bitmaps are the standard Windows image format and only support RGB color and bit depths of 1, 4, 8, or 24 bits per channel. These attributes make them unsuitable for professional imaging. File size is high, which also makes them unsuitable for web use.

JPEG – this format is suitable for virtually all types of application as it supports RGB, CMYK, and grayscale color spaces. Its main feature is the fact that it can be highly compressed with no noticeable loss of quality (up to a point). This makes it ideal for use in web pages, and where a low file size is required. It can also handle 24-bit color, which makes it suitable for professional use. Pictures downloaded from most digital cameras will be in this format. JPEG is the best all-round format.

When saving an image as a JPEG, any imaging program will use a default level of compression. This will reduce the size of the file considerably with no noticeable loss in quality. However, if you want to set the level of compression yourself, look for an "Options" button. This will open a dialog box from where you can set the compression level using a slider.

TIFF – a TIFF is a raster-based file that supports RGB, CMYK, Grayscale, Lab, and Indexed color. TIFF files are high in size and are really only suitable for professional publishing.

Streaming is the real-time transmission of video from the Internet that allows the user to watch a movie without having to first download the entire file to the computer.

Video

Video formats are basically "containers" into which the video and audio data is placed. The data is then compressed with a suitable codec. This is necessary because in its raw state a video file can be so enormous as to be impractical.

The most commonly used video formats are:

AVI – AVI is typically used for low-quality video clips, and is commonly found on multimedia CD-ROMs, such as encyclopedias. As AVI does not offer high compression rates, file sizes are high; this makes it unsuitable for high-resolution video. AVI files are, however, easy to edit.

MPEG (MPG) – MPEG is actually a container and codec rolled into one, and is available in several versions – MPEG-1, MPEG-2 and MPEG-4. This is the most commonly used video format. The first, MPEG-1 is typically used for multimedia discs such as encyclopedias. Video quality is reasonable.
The second, MPEG-2, produces broadcast-quality video, with the added advantage of low file sizes due to superior compression techniques; commercial DVDs use this format.
The third, MPEG-4, has been designed specifically for video streaming from the Internet (see top margin note).

Do not confuse codecs with file formats; they are not the same. A video format is a frame which contains the data. A codec reduces the size of the data by compressing it.

Popular codecs are:

- *DivX – An extremely advanced codec that makes it possible to download a full-screen broadcast-quality movie from the Internet*

- *MPEG-2 – Produces broadcast-quality video with the added advantage of low file sizes*

- *Xvid – this is an open-source codec, meaning that anyone can develop their own version. Similar to DivX*

QuickTime – this is Apple's video format standard, and is similar to Microsoft's AVI format in both functionality and quality. The latest version (QuickTime-7) also enables video streaming. Many digital cameras produce small video clips in this format.

ASF – this is a Microsoft format designed for the streaming of video and is not really suitable for any other purpose. Having said that, it's not uncommon to find small ASF video clips on the Internet.

RM – this format is used by RealPlayer, a media player marketed by RealNetworks. To play an RM file, RealPlayer must be installed on the PC. Other media players, such as Windows Media Player, do not support this format.

How to Create a Movie CD/DVD

Before you can start digitizing those old VHS holiday movies, you need some method of importing the video to the PC. If your system has a video card with capturing facilities, just connect the VCR to the card's VIVO port.

If you have a video camera that uses compatible VHS tapes, you can use that. Otherwise, you will have to invest in a video capture card.

You will need special software to create a movie disc. Programs such as "Ulead VideoStudio," "Pinnacle Studio" and "Sonic MyDVD Studio," have all the functions required for the entire operation, including burning the disc.

Other editing programs might only be able to create certain types of disc, and might not have burning facilities.

So before you start, make sure you have all the necessary tools.

Making your own DVD movies is a simple, if time consuming process. The procedure involves the following steps:

- Capturing the video from the source to the hard drive
- Editing the video
- Encoding the video
- Authoring (DVDs and SVCDs)
- Burning to disk

The first step is to get the raw material onto your hard drive. If it has been recorded with a video camera, all you have to do is connect the camera to the PC. Then open your authoring software and find the Import button.

If the source is a video recorder, you will need a video capturing device. This can be a TV tuner card, a video card with integral video capturing facilities, or a dedicated capture card.

Having imported the raw footage, you then need to edit it. What you do here is entirely up to you, but as a general rule you want to avoid unexpected jumps from one scene to another. To this end, the editing software will provide transition effects, such as wipes, fades and curls.

When you've finished editing, the movie must be encoded to a suitable file format.

Here, you have the following choices:

For the best possible video quality, you need to use the DVD format. This will give you a high-resolution, full-screen display. In addition, you will also be able to add interactive features, such as chapters and menus.

- VCD (VideoCD) – this provides reasonable quality and can be played in most home DVD players, in all home VCD players, and in all CD-ROM drives. The file format used is MPEG-1. Video dimensions are 352 x 240.

- SVCD (SuperVCD) – this produces higher quality video but a disc will hold only about 35 to 40 minutes of video (as opposed to 75 minutes with the VCD format). In addition, just like DVD, SVCD discs can also contain subtitles, still images, multi-level hierarchical menus, chapters, hyperlinks, and play lists. Video dimensions are 480 x 480. SVCDs can be played in most DVD players and all VCD players. The file format used is MPEG-2.

The software will also offer "Save As" options, such as AVI and Multimedia. These will produce low-quality video, and also small picture dimensions. These options are not recommended.

- DVD (Digital Video Disc) – DVD discs use the MPEG2 format and produce the highest quality video. Video dimensions are 720 x 480. Discs will play in all DVD players. As with SVCD discs, chapters, hyperlinks and play lists, etc, are possible with DVD.

Make your selection and press the Make Movie button. When this is done, if you've chosen SVCD or DVD, you now need to create the menus, chapters, subtitles, etc. You will find plenty of suitable templates in your editing program, as shown below.

Creating movies on a PC is a resource intensive operation and will require a well-specified system (no less than 512 MB of RAM). Try doing it with less and you will find it an extremely slow and painful procedure.

You will also need plenty of hard drive space, as video files can be enormous.

Finally, burn the movie to a disc.

Get the Best Out of Your Games

Before buying any 3D game, make sure your CPU and RAM match its recommended system requirements. These will be somewhere on the box. You must also have the version of DirectX required by the game; otherwise it won't run properly, if at all.

The average computer system is not specified highly enough to play many of today's 3D games at their optimum level. By this we mean all sound/graphic enhancements and features turned on and set at maximum. With "all guns blazing," many of the games will struggle, with gameplay being slow and jerky. If you experience this, try doing the following in the order specified:

1) Reinstall the game and choose the option that installs the majority of the game's data on the hard drive. The less the game has to access the CD, the smoother the gameplay.

2) Before you start the game, switch off for a few seconds. Doing this will clear the memory and ensure the PC is in a stable condition.

Achieving a smooth level of gameplay is usually a compromise between graphics quality and performance, and will require a certain amount of trial and error.

3) When playing the game make sure no other applications are running, particularly anti-virus and disk utilities.

4) Try reducing the amount of action, i.e. reduce the number of opponents, cars in a racing game, etc. The less that is going on, the less required of the PC.

5) Go into the game's graphics setup options and reduce the screen-resolution. Then reduce settings such as Anti-Aliasing, Shadows, and Textures. These features improve graphic quality enormously but place a heavy load on the PC.

If the game's installation options allow you to install the entire game to the hard drive, do so. Having to constantly retrieve data from the CD-ROM drive will inevitably cause the game to stutter.

Graphics options for MotoCross Madness 2. Dragging the sliders down will speed up the game

6) The final option is to upgrade your system's RAM, and possibly the CPU and video system as well.

Disable Media Content Protection

Don't forget the legal aspect to this. All music is copyrighted and this expressly forbids copying and distribution. Sharing your music with others is an illegal activity.

Many people use their PCs to copy music to and from CDs. This is, or should be, for their own use. It's a popular pastime.

However, users who are accustomed to doing this may discover a problem when they attempt do it with XP's Media Player. This is due to a feature of this utility known as "Content Protection." What this does is to prevent music files created with Media Player on one computer from being played on another.

So before you burn a load of music to a writable CD, make sure Content Protection is turned off (it is enabled by default). Do it as follows:

1 On Media Player's menu bar, go to Tools, Options

2 Click the Copy Music tab and then remove the check mark from the Protect content box

Now you will be able to make recordings that can be played on a different computer.

Create a PC Entertainment Center

Quite apart from analog TV, high-end tuner cards can also receive free-to-air digital TV and full-quality free-to-air HDTV. It's also worth pointing out that digital TV produced by tuner cards is superior to that produced by a standard digital TV.

The unique switching, storage and control features of a computer makes it possible to create a PC-based home entertainment center that is far superior to the motley collection of TVs, VHS recorders, DVD players and stereo systems found in many homes. To build one, apart from the PC itself, you will need the following:

- a CD-ROM drive for playing audio CDs
- a DVD drive for playing commercially produced movies
- a TV tuner
- a DVD decoder
- a set of quality speakers (a Surround-Sound system ideally)

These parts will form a basic entertainment center that will enable you to watch and record TV, listen to music, and watch DVD movies. Furthermore, they will all be accessible (and able to be controlled) from a central point (the PC).

Another option is to install Microsoft's "Plus Digital Media Edition." This is basically a set of tools and utilities that adds some new features and several enhancements to the existing XP platform. An example is a utility that will enable you to record from an analog source, such as tape or vinyl; this includes an inbuilt noise reduction feature to remove background hiss and pops from scratches on vinyl or tape recordings.

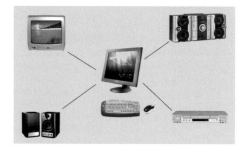

You also have the option of using existing standalone devices (stereo systems, VHS recorders, DVD players, etc.). To do this though, you will need a sound card, and also a video card, with the necessary inputs and outputs with which to connect the devices to the PC.

Rather than buying a separate TV tuner and hardware DVD decoder, buy a video card that has both integrated on the board. This will also increase your options regarding standalone devices by providing the necessary inputs and outputs.

With a suitable video card and a wide-screen LCD monitor, your entertainment center will also feature a high-definition TV.

Another very useful option is provided by a device known as a "Digital Media Adapter." This provides a wireless connection that will allow you to send/receive sound, video and images to and from any device, wherever it is in the house.

Security

There are several aspects to security in a computer – the main one being the prevention of unauthorized access. Unfortunately, XP's security levels has proved to be one of its greatest failings, and so the greater part of this chapter is devoted to showing how to make a PC running XP as secure as possible.

Covers

Chapter Seven

Secure the PC Against Attack

Windows XP is riddled with security holes that leave it wide open to malicious attack by hackers and viruses. Implementing the steps on pages 88-91 will help to keep your computer secure.

Install Service Pack 2

This security update plugs many of the loopholes in Internet Explorer and Outlook Express (it's via these two applications that the vast majority of viruses and worms get onto a PC).

The main change to Internet Explorer is that file downloads can only happen if initiated by the user (previously a website could download a file without the user's knowledge). If a website attempts to do this with SP2, the download is blocked and a yellow information bar (shown below) appears, offering various options. By clicking the bar, you are given the option to download the file if you think it's safe to do so.

SP2 also includes several security enhancements to Outlook Express that reduce the possibility of downloading a virus concealed in an email.

Run a Firewall

A personal computer connected to the Internet without a firewall can be hijacked in literally minutes by automated hacking programs.

Running a PC without one these days is like going out for the day and leaving the front door wide open. Fortunately, XP supplies a firewall. If you don't have SP2 installed, enable it by going to Start, Control Panel and Network Connections.

XP's firewall, while adequate, is not the best of its type. Its main failing is that it doesn't prevent data leaving the PC, whereas better firewalls, such as Zone Alarm, will. So, should a hacker manage to gain access to your PC and plant something nasty, XP's firewall will not be able to prevent it sending your data back to the hacker.

The advice, therefore, is to install a better firewall that provides two-way protection and then disable XP's firewall.

The professional version of XP provides many more security features than the home edition does. One of the best of these is the Encrypted File System (EFS). EFS provides automatic data encryption for files and folders. Data encrypted by EFS can be accessed only by the user who encrypted them.

Right-click your Internet connection, click Properties, the Advanced tab and finally the Internet Connection Firewall (if you have SP2 installed, the firewall will be enabled by default).

Run an Anti-Virus Program

This applies particularly if you do a lot of downloading from the Internet and receive email. Whichever program you use, make sure it is regularly updated.

Turn on Automatic Updates

This feature automatically downloads updates and fixes to XP as and when they are released. It is particularly important to enable this utility if you haven't installed SP2. Do it as follows:

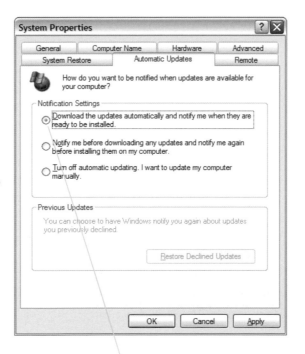

Go to Start, Control Panel, System. Click the Automatic Updates tab

2 Tick "Download the updates automatically and notify me when they are ready to be installed"

When configuring XP's automatic updates, you also have the option of making it notify you before it downloads any updates.

Password-Protect Your Accounts

In most single-user environments, password-protection is not enabled as there is no apparent need for it. However, should a hacker gain access to the PC, any accounts that are not password protected will be wide open. For this reason, if you want to make your PC as secure as possible, you must assign a password to *all* the accounts on the system.

Do it as follows:

By default, all user accounts created in Windows XP will not have a password set for them. This makes them easily accessible to all and sundry. To keep your data safe from hackers and anyone else who may be nosing about, you must set a password for all the computer's accounts.

1 Go to Start, Control Panel, User Accounts

2 Click Change an Account and in the next dialog box, click the account to be protected

Hackers use automated (brute force) software to crack passwords. Commonly used passwords such as the user's name, sequential keystrokes such as QUERTY, and common words, will be cracked in no time.

Use the following rules to set a strong password:

1) *Use at least 8 characters*

2) *Use a mix of upper case, lower case, and numeric characters*

3) *Use ALT characters. These are characters produced by holding down the ALT key and typing on the keyboard's numeric keypad*

3 Click Create a Password

4 Enter the password

Carry out the above procedure for all the user accounts that have been created on the PC.

Simply turning off the Guest account will not be sufficient, since it will only be turned off in terms of its ability to logon directly to Windows. In the background, the account will still be functional because XP uses it to authenticate users connecting remotely to shared resources on the PC. It is virtually impossible to truly disable the Guest account, and doing so would cause a number of problems.

When you get to the Guest account, you will find there is no option to assign a password. So do it as described below:

1   Open a command prompt window by going to Start, All Programs, Accessories, Command Prompt

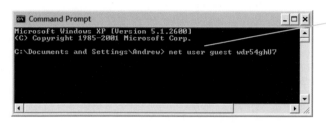

2   Type net user guest followed by the password

3   Press Enter, and the Guest account password will be set

Finally, you must set a password for the default Administrator account. This account is hidden and does not show up in User Accounts (except in Safe Mode) or the Welcome Screen. Very few people are aware this account even exists – hackers do though.

By default, the default Administrator account is hidden. However, anyone who knows this, and can gain access to it, will have full administrator privileges. This will allow them to do whatever they like. Password-protecting this account will reduce the possibility of this happening.

1   Go to Start, Run. In the Run box, type the following:

control userpasswords2

The Administrator account can be accessed in User Accounts by starting the PC in Safe Mode.

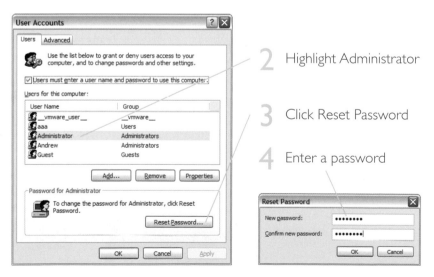

2   Highlight Administrator

3   Click Reset Password

4   Enter a password

Password-Protect Your Folders

XP provides two methods of doing this:

The first is by "Making a folder private." Do it by right-clicking the folder, selecting Properties and clicking the Sharing tab.

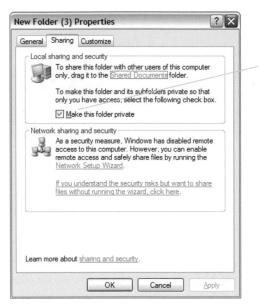

Tick the "Make this folder private" box (in some circumstances the option will be grayed out (see top margin note)

The second way is by creating a compressed folder. Right-click the Desktop and select New, Compressed (zipped) folder.

Open the compressed folder and from the File menu select Add a Password

2 Enter a password

...cont'd

The tip on this page will only work on password-protected user accounts. To unlock the PC you will need the password for the account in question.

In step 2 opposite, note the space between "exe" and "user." The command must be typed in exactly as written.

If you have Fast User Switching enabled, instead of getting the "This computer is in use and has been locked" dialog box, you will be taken to the logon screen. The effect will be the same though; the PC will be locked and will need the account password to unlock it.

While this tip doesn't hide the contents of the folder, it does make it impossible to access the files within without entering the password.

Lock The Computer Quickly

An occasion might arise when you are in the middle of an important task on the computer, when for some reason, you are called away in a hurry for what will probably be a short period. You haven't got time to save the work and switch off, but you don't want to leave it unattended in case someone comes along and meddles with it while you're away.

There is a quick and foolproof way round this problem:

1   Right-click the Desktop, select New and then Shortcut

2   In the Location of item box, type the following:

      rundll32.exe user32.dll,LockWorkStation

3   Click Next and in the next dialog box, give the shortcut a suitable name. Then click OK

If you don't want to go to the bother of creating a special icon to lock the computer, you can achieve the same thing by simply pressing the Windows key on the keyboard in conjunction with the letter L.

4   To lock the PC instantly, simply click the shortcut's icon

Create an Encrypted Password Disk

This tip provides an extremely secure method of locking a PC by using an encrypted key.

<u>WARNING</u>: This procedure cannot be undone. Be quite sure that you need this level of security before you start.

Do it as described below:

Once done, password encryption cannot be undone. If you should lose the key, you will have to use a repair disk to restore the Registry to a state prior to password encryption protection being enabled. Any changes to the PC that were made after that time will be lost.

| Go to Start, Run and in the box type syskey

2 In the next dialog box, click Update

While the tip on this page provides an extremely strong method of securing a PC, it will only be so as long as the disk itself is secure. Should it fall into the wrong hands then it's actually an open invitation. Furthermore, should it be lost or become damaged, then you will be locked out of your own PC.

In your own interests, make a couple of backup copies of the disk.

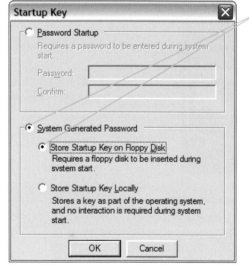

3 Select "System Generated Password" and then "Store Startup Key on Floppy Disk"

4 You will now be asked to insert a floppy disk after which an encrypted key will be saved to the disk

From this point, every time the computer is started, you will be asked to insert the disk into the floppy drive before you can access the logon screen. So just make sure you don't lose it, otherwise you won't be able to access your own computer.

Keep Your Account Password Safe

It is a fact that passwords are notoriously easy to forget, particularly if you have set passwords for several different computer applications. You may actually have quite a few to remember.

In the case of your user account, XP gives you an option for saving your password in case you forget it.

Keep your password-reset disk in a safe place. If someone else gets hold of it, they will be able to access your account by setting a new password that will supersede the previous one. You will then be unable to access your own account.

1 Go to Start, Control Panel, User Accounts. Click the account the password for which you wish to save. In the new dialog box you'll see a range of options, including (on the far left) Related Tasks

2 Click Prevent a forgotten password

Many of us take advantage of Windows' ability to remember passwords and enter them automatically. As a result, very often, we forget what they are. However, there are utilities that can read the password behind the row of asterisks in a password box. One such is "Asterisk Key" available from www.LostPassword.com.

3 The Forgotten Password wizard launches – simply follow the prompts

4 If you enter the incorrect password when logging on, a pop-up message will appear saying "Did you forget your password? You can use your password-reset disk"

Click "Use your password-reset disk" and a recovery wizard will prompt you to insert the disk in the floppy drive. You will now be able to set a new password that will replace the original one

How to Hide Private Folders

There are any number of reasons why someone might wish to hide a folder. It might, for example, contain important work documents or a set of financial accounts.

It is possible to password-protect a folder in XP Home (see page 92). However, it doesn't actually hide the folder itself, and so anyone who comes across it, while they won't be able to access it, will know it probably contains something important. In effect, it's been "signposted" as such. The point here is that to someone in the know, there are methods of cracking passwords.

Another way to hide a folder is to simply squirrel it away in a folder containing a mass of other folders or sub-folders. Just don't forget where it is.

Another option is to simply conceal the existence of the folder, and this can be done as follows:

1 Right-click the folder to be hidden and select Properties. Click the General tab and tick the Hidden box

2 Open any folder, and from the menu bar select Tools, Folder Options. In the new dialog box, click the View tab

The method described on this page, while useful, is by no means a secure one. Anyone who knows how to access hidden folders will be able to access your hidden ones as well.

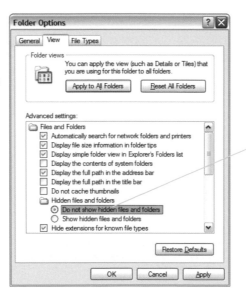

3 Select Do not show hidden files or folders

The next time the drive containing your folder is opened, the folder will not be visible. To access it, simply undo step 3 above.

Hide Your Browsing Tracks

There is any number of reasons why someone might not want others to know what sites they have been accessing on the Internet. There is also the possibility of stumbling across some of the Internet's less salubrious content in all innocence (there can't be many people who haven't).

The problem is that Internet Explorer keeps a record of what you have been getting up to on the Internet. To remove this record and thus hide your browsing tracks, there are five things you must do:

Don't forget to check your Internet Favorites. When accessed, certain sites will automatically place a link to their site here. Common culprits in this respect are porn sites. Your Internet Favorites can be accessed from the menu bar in most windows, and anyone who happens to do this will see anything which has been added in this way (innocently or otherwise).

1) Delete the contents of the Cookies folder (this can be found at Documents and Settings\User name\Cookies). Cookies are small text files that many sites automatically download to your PC, the purpose of which is to identify you should you visit that site again. Often, they will also identify the type of site, e.g. stuart@luckydollarcasino.

2) Delete the contents of the History folder (Documents and settings\User name\Local Settings). This folder is used by Internet Explorer to keep a record of all the websites you have visited.

3) Delete the contents of the Temporary Internet Files folder (Documents and Settings\User name\Local Settings). This folder is basically a cache of the pages you have accessed. Should you revisit a particular site, instead of pulling it off the Web, your browser will retrieve it from this cache. This makes access to the page much quicker.

The three folders that can give the game away for you are the Temporary Internet Files folder, the History folder and the Cookies folder.

4) Check your Internet Favorites. Some sites will place a link here without advising you of the fact.

5) Disable AutoComplete – see page 99.

Anyone (who knows how) can access the above mentioned folders and see exactly what you have been doing on the Internet. One way to prevent this is to open each of the folders and manually delete their contents at the end of each browsing session.

There is, however, an easier way:

You can configure Internet Explorer to automatically clear the Temporary Internet Files folder when it is closed.

1) Open Internet Options

2) Click the Advanced tab

3) Scroll down to "Empty Temporary Internet Files folder when browser is closed" and tick the box

When you change your privacy settings, the changes may not affect cookies that are already on your computer. To ensure that all the cookies on your computer meet your privacy settings, you must first delete all the existing cookies.

Be wary of choosing too high a privacy setting. If you do, you will find that certain web pages will not function correctly. A typical example is pages containing a password logon box; these may not load at all.

1 Go to Start, Control Panel, Internet Options

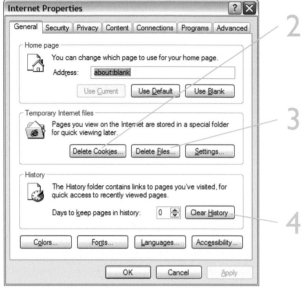

2 Delete all existing Cookies here

3 Delete Temporary Internet files here

4 Clear the History folder by clicking here

5 Click the Privacy tab

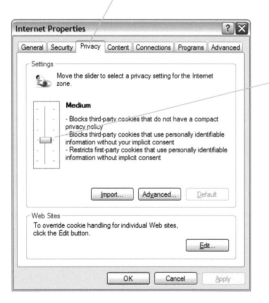

6 Using the slider, you can adjust the types of Cookie that your browser will accept

Turn Off AutoComplete

Internet Explorer has a feature called AutoComplete, which when enabled causes the browser to automatically enter web addresses, user-names, passwords, and data entered on web-based forms. This can be convenient as it saves the user from having to type out this information each time.

Be careful when using AutoComplete. Not only can it automatically enter your passwords and user-names for other people to use illicitly, it can also enable people to see exactly what sites you have been visiting and what keywords you have been entering in search engine search boxes.

However, it can also be dangerous, as potentially, it allows other people to access your password-protected pages and see what data you've entered in forms, etc. It will also enable any snooper to see exactly what websites you have visited and any keywords entered in search engine search boxes.

If you wish to keep this type of information private then you need to disable AutoComplete or alter its settings. This can be done as follows:

The safest way to use AutoComplete is to disable the "User names and passwords on forms" option. Enabling it to remember web addresses is safe and can be very useful.

1 Go to Start, Control Panel, Internet Options. Click the Content tab

Disabling any of AutoComplete's settings, as in step 3, will also remove any information it previously held regarding the setting.

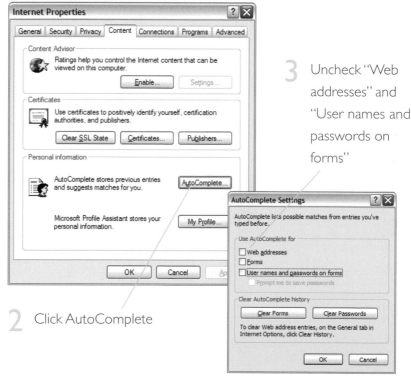

3 Uncheck "Web addresses" and "User names and passwords on forms"

2 Click AutoComplete

Censor Web Content

In order to outwit your kids, who are probably more computer savvy than you are, you can password-protect the settings you make in Content Advisor. To do this, click the General Tab and then click the Create Password button.

Many people, with good reason, are wary of letting their children loose on the Internet unsupervised. There can't be many who aren't aware of the dangers posed by chatrooms and various other types of sites.

So the responsible parent will want to be sure their children are not accessing things they shouldn't be. How to do it though?

One way is to sit with them, which can be excruciating if all they want to do is catch up with the latest adventures of their favorite popstar, for example.

A less painful way is to make use of XP's Content Advisor, which is available from Internet Options under the Content tab. Click Enable to see what options are available.

XP's Content Advisor is not the best application of its type. For example, setting the ratings slider too high will often block access to completely innocuous sites. Much better programs include "Net Nanny" and "Cyber Patrol."

Drag the slider to set the level of permissible content

A more useful part of Content Advisor is its Approved Sites feature. This allows you to block access to specific sites and allow access to others.

2 Click the Approved Sites tab to specify accessible sites

Installation/Setting Up

There comes a time in the life of any PC when the operating system needs to be reinstalled – this chapter shows you how to do it with XP.

There are also several features of XP, such as dual booting and disk management, that need to be correctly configured in order to achieve the desired result.

Covers

Chapter Eight

Trouble-free XP Reinstallation

Before carrying out a Windows reinstallation, make sure you have backed up any data you don't wish to lose. While it's rare, an installation can result in the loss of data.

A Windows reinstallation is usually done when the existing copy has a serious problem that the user is unable to resolve. This will usually be due to missing or damaged system files.

Although XP will normally reinstall without any problems, there will always be occasions when it doesn't. This isn't due to anything inherently wrong with XP's installation program, but will usually be the result of the user not taking a few simple precautionary measures beforehand.

So before you do a reinstallation of XP, do the following:

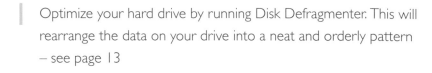

1 Optimize your hard drive by running Disk Defragmenter. This will rearrange the data on your drive into a neat and orderly pattern – see page 13

It is important to uninstall or disable any anti-virus software you have on your system before reinstalling XP.

2 Run Chkdsk to check your hard drive. Drive errors are a common cause of failed installations – see page 21

3 Check the system for the presence of viruses and malware – see page 25. These can stop an installation in its tracks

4 Having ascertained that your system is free of viruses, uninstall the anti-virus program. Alternatively, disable it via the BIOS setup program. These programs are a common cause of installation problems

When carrying out a reinstallation, although not essential, it is a good idea to disconnect as much of your system hardware as you can. Examples are printers, scanners and modems. The reason for this is that it is during the hardware detection and configuration stages of an installation that problems often occur.

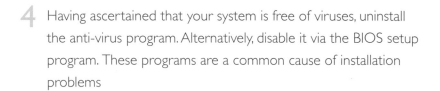

5 Disable or uninstall any applications that run in the background and can suddenly activate. Examples are screensavers, anti-virus programs and utility programs such as Norton's System Works

6 Remove all programs from your Startup folder – see page 30

Carrying out the above steps will almost certainly enable you to reinstall XP without a hitch.

How to do a Clean XP Installation

The BIOS setup program is accessed by switching on the computer, and as the first boot screen loads, holding down a key. This is usually the Delete key but some BIOSes may require a different key. This is specified at the bottom of the boot screen.

When installing any version of Windows, you have two ways to do it. The first is to simply install over the existing version. This can be a reinstallation (as described on the previous page to correct a problem), or an upgrade to a new version of Windows.

The second option is to do a clean installation and is definitely the better of the two. This is because the hard drive has to be formatted first, and this procedure literally wipes the drive clean. When a system is badly infected with viruses, spyware, hijackers and the like, a clean installation is the only way that's guaranteed to get rid of them all. Do it with XP as follows:

1 Backup all data you wish to keep to a second hard drive or writable CD

2 Start the PC and access the BIOS Setup program (see top margin note). Open the Advanced BIOS Features page and scroll down to First Boot Device

With Windows XP, the installation CD is the boot disk. This means that you have to set the CD-ROM drive as the first boot device. Earlier versions of Windows operating systems need a boot floppy disk for installation. This disk contains the partitioning and formatting tools, plus a generic CD-ROM driver.

XP provides everything you need on the installation disk.

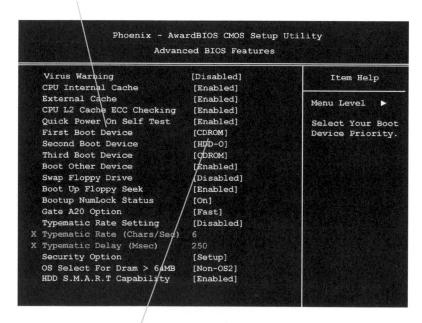

3 Using the Page Up/Page Down keys, select CDROM, save the change and exit the BIOS

The "Press any key to boot from CD....." message is displayed only for five seconds at the bottom of the boot screen. If necessary, you can press the Pause key which will stop boot-up until you've found it.

Having set the CD-ROM drive as the first boot device, place the XP installation disk in the CD drive and boot the PC. At the bottom of the second boot screen, you will see a message saying "Press any key to boot from CD.....". Do so, and after a short period, you'll see the following screen:

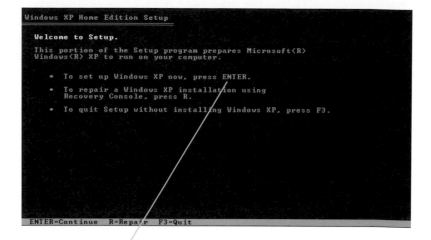

4   Hit Enter to begin the XP installation

```
Windows XP Licensing Agreement

  Microsoft Windows XP Home Edition

  END-USER LICENSE AGREEMENT

  IMPORTANT-READ CAREFULLY: This End-User
  License Agreement ("EULA") is a legal agreement between you
  (either an individual or a single entity) and Microsoft
  Corporation for the Microsoft software product identified above,
  which includes computer software and may include associated
  media, printed materials, "online" or electronic documentation,
  and Internet-based services ("Product").   An amendment or
  addendum to this EULA may accompany the Product.  YOU AGREE TO BE
  BOUND BY THE TERMS OF THIS EULA BY
  INSTALLING, COPYING, OR OTHERWISE USING THE
  PRODUCT.  IF YOU DO NOT AGREE, DO NOT INSTALL
  OR USE THE PRODUCT; YOU MAY RETURN IT TO YOUR
  PLACE OF PURCHASE FOR A FULL REFUND.

    1. GRANT OF LICENSE. Microsoft grants you the following rights
       provided that you comply with all terms and conditions of
       this EULA:

       * Installation and use.  You may install, use, access,
         display and run one copy of the Product on a single
         computer, such as a workstation, terminal or other device
         ("Workstation Computer").   [a] The Product may not
         be used by more than one (1) processor at any one time

 F8=I agree   ESC=I do not agree   PAGE DOWN=Next Page
```

5   First though, you need to accept the licence agreement by pressing the F8 key

If you already have an operating system on the system, you will need to delete the partition on which it is installed. You can do this in step 7 by pressing D on the keyboard. Then press Enter to create a new single partition. Alternatively, you can create two or more partitions as described in step 9 on page 106.

6 If you are using an upgrade version, then you'll need to prove that you have owned a full version of Windows at some point by placing it in the CD drive. Otherwise, you won't see this screen

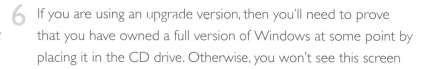
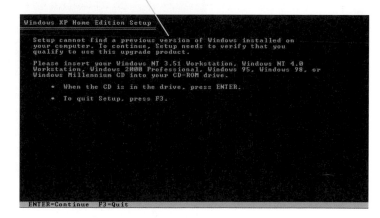

If you are installing XP (Home or Professional) with an upgrade CD, be sure to have your qualifying media to hand. This can be a retail Windows 98, 98 SE, Millennium Edition (ME), NT 4.0 or 2000 CD-ROM.

7 Next, you will see a screen showing available installation options (drives/partitions where XP can be installed). If you are installing to a new hard drive, it won't yet have a partition; in this case, you will see unpartitioned space equivalent to the drive's size

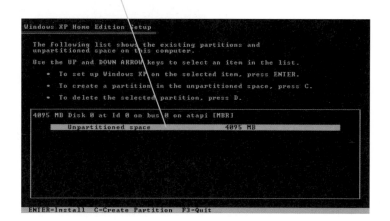

If you are unfamiliar with partitioning procedures, accept XP's default partition setting, i.e. one partition equal to the full size of the disk.

At this stage, you have two options. First, if you press Enter, XP will automatically create a single partition equal to the size of the drive. If you do this, you will then be taken directly to the format screen as shown on the next page.

XP allows you to format the drive in one of two file systems – NTFS or FAT. Unless you are planning to make use of XP's dual boot facility that allows two or more operating systems to be installed on the PC, choose the NTFS option; this will be the best choice.

You also have the option of doing a "Quick" format. Only use this if the drive is new, as this option does not check the disk for errors such as bad sectors.

8 Select the file system you want to use – FAT or NTFS – and press Enter. XP will then format the newly created partition

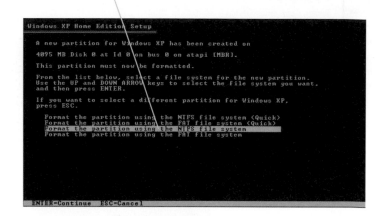

However, if you want to create two or more partitions, then press "C" in Step 7 on page 105. You will see the partitioning screen shown below.

The "Quick" format option will take a few seconds literally. The "Full" format option, however, can take a long time. The larger the drive's capacity, the longer it will take.

9 Here, you can create partitions in sizes of your own choice. When done, press Enter to go to the Format screen (step 8 above)

Once the disk has been partitioned and formatted, the installation routine will automatically begin copying files to the hard drive. All you have to do now is follow the prompts until the installation is complete.

Dual Booting With XP

If you have only one hard drive in your system then you will need to partition it. The simplest way to do this is with a partition utility such as Powerquest's Partition Magic. However, if you don't have this, XP supplies you with all the tools you need, although it will be a more long-winded process.

With XP's dual boot facility, Microsoft have for the first time given users the opportunity to run two or more operating systems on the same computer without the need for third-party software.

However, before you attempt to do this there are a few ground rules you ought to familiarize yourself with.

Each operating system must be installed to a separate hard drive. However, even if you have only one drive, you can still dual boot; in this case you must split the drive to create two or more partitions, each of which will appear as a separate drive to Windows. See the top margin note and also page 106.

There are also limitations on which combination of Windows versions you can dual boot with XP. The main one concerns Windows 95, 98 and ME: You can only have one of these systems dual booting with XP.

Non-Microsoft operating systems will not work with XP's boot manager.

You cannot have more than one instance of Windows 95, 98 or ME in a multiboot environment. You can only use one of these systems.

The table below shows possible dual boot configurations:

- MS-DOS
- Windows 95 or Windows 98 or Windows ME
- Windows NT
- Windows 2000
- Windows XP (Home or Professional)

Having decided which systems you wish to install, the next thing you must do is install them in the correct order.

The rule is that you install your chosen systems in order of age, beginning with the oldest. XP (either Home or Pro) is the system you install last. An example setup is shown below:

- Windows 98 – installed first on Drive C
- Windows 2000 – installed second on Drive D
- Windows XP – installed last on Drive E

If you follow the above rules then you will be able to successfully dual boot with XP. Do it any other way and you will find it an extremely frustrating experience.

Setting the Default Boot System

XP's boot manager is a somewhat basic example of this type of program. There are many other, much better boot managers on the market. A good example is PowerQuest's Boot Magic. Amongst other features, this program allows operating systems on the boot menu to be password-protected.

This tip is for those who have set up their computer as a dual boot system with two or more operating systems. When this has been done, and the computer is started, they will be presented with a boot menu which shows the available operating systems. These are selected by using the arrow keys.

The system at the top of the list is the default system, and if the user hasn't made a choice within a specified number of seconds, is the one that the PC will run.

Should the user wish to set a different system as the default, this is the way to do it:

Right-click My Computer, click Properties, click the Advanced tab and then click the Settings button under Startup and Recovery

Be extremely wary of using a third-party Disk Manager with a dual boot setup. These applications are used to overcome a limitation with some BIOSes that prevents a hard drive's full capacity being recognized. When used with a single operating system setup, they present no problem, but on a dual boot setup, they can cause major problems, such as failure to boot-up and total loss of a drive's data.

2 The drop-down box will show the operating systems installed. Select the one you want to be the default and click OK

3 You can also change the time available to make your choice in this dialog box

Set up XP for Several Users

XP allows the setting up of any number of user accounts, each of which can be individually configured in many ways (Desktop icons, wallpapers, screensavers, etc).

XP's user accounts enable a PC to be personalized for any number of different users. They can each set up their account as they would if it was their own PC.

This feature is particularly useful in a home environment where several family members all use the PC. By giving each their own account, which they can customize to suit their specific requirements and tastes, a single PC can be used sensibly and without conflict.

It can also be useful in a single-user environment by enabling a user to create accounts for specific purposes. For example, one account can be set up for video-editing with shortcuts to all the relevant programs placed on the Desktop. Another account can be set up as a home office, etc.

User accounts are set up as follows:

When more than one account is created, one of those accounts must be an Administrator account. The person running this account will be able to set restrictions on what other account holders can and cannot do. For example, restrictions can be placed on which folders can be accessed and whether or not programs can be installed or uninstalled.

1   Go to Start, Control Panel, User Accounts

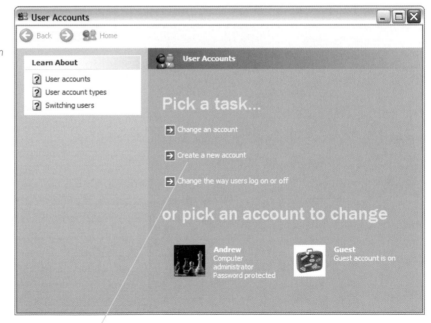

2   Click Create a new account

...cont'd

Limited accounts are intended for users who are not allowed to change the computer settings and delete important files. Some of the limitations that apply to limited accounts are:

- *Software and hardware cannot be installed. However, programs that have already been installed can be used*

- *Account names and types cannot be changed*

- *Only settings within the account can be changed. System-wide changes are not allowed*

3 Give the account a name

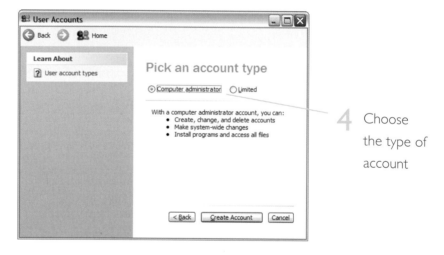

4 Choose the type of account

Guest accounts are similar to limited accounts. These allow the computer to be used but no important settings can be changed. In addition, guest users cannot access the Internet via a dial-up connection.

Accounts can be either administrator, limited or guest. An administrator has full control over the PC, and in a home environment this type of account will be given to someone who can be trusted to not use it in an irresponsible manner.

A limited account means just what it says. For example, a person using a limited account cannot install/uninstall hardware or software. Typically, these accounts are for the kids.

Guest accounts are the most restricted of all and are suitable for the babysitter.

Don't Lose Your Old Files & Settings

If you don't possess a backup medium of suitable capacity but can establish a network connection to your new PC, you can use this method to transfer your files and settings.

One of these days you're going to decide that you need a new computer. Having bought it, you will then need to reinstall all your programs. You will also need to redo all the customization and configuration settings, such as Internet/email settings, Display settings, Taskbar configuration and so on. The latter can be a time consuming procedure.

XP makes this easy with its Files and Settings Transfer Wizard. However, in order to use it you will need a transfer medium such as a network, or direct cable connection. Alternatively, a high-capacity drive medium such as a Zip disk or writable CD can be used.

Don't try to transfer files by using floppy disks as the medium; they simply do not have the capacity. However, they will be quite adequate for transferring system settings, which should fit on one disk, two at most.

1 Insert the XP installation disk in the CD-ROM drive of the old PC, and when it runs, select Perform Additional Tasks from the menu

2 In the new dialog box, select Transfer Files and Settings

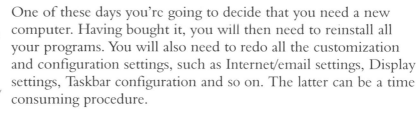

The Files and Settings Transfer Wizard allows you to move settings and files from PCs running Windows 9x, ME, 2000, NT 4.0 and XP.

3 The Files and Settings Transfer Wizard will open

The Files and Settings Transfer Wizard will not transfer your applications. These will need to be manually installed on the new computer.

4 Follow the prompts until you see a message telling you that this part of the procedure is finished and that you must now go to the new computer

5 At the new PC, run the Wizard again and simply follow the prompts until the transfer is complete

Read the Instructions

At the risk of stating the obvious, do read the documentation supplied with software and hardware devices.

System Requirements

The main resources that a computer program/device needs are processor power and memory (RAM).

Many installation disks, in addition to the main program, will also contain other applications which require manual installation. Some of these can be very useful programs in their own right and are well worth installing.

An example is TV tuner cards, disks for which often contain video-editing programs not installed by default

So dig out all those installation disks and have a look inside them. You will be surprised at what you find.

Before you buy a program/device therefore, study the packaging, and somewhere you'll see the manufacturer's recommended minimum system requirements. If your system doesn't match these, put it back on the shelf, you'll just be wasting money otherwise. This also applies to XP itself, and many people are blithely buying it on the assumption that it will work because their previous versions did. Unfortunately, in many cases they are finding out differently.

"Readme" Files

Somewhere, on virtually any installation disk, there will be a Notepad, Internet Explorer or Word document detailing system requirements as mentioned above. In addition, there will usually also be a "Readme" or "Setup" file, which will give installation and setting up instructions. There may also be a section regarding known compatibility issues or "bugs" as they are called. This will give details of hardware devices which might not work with the program/device. Do read these files as they can save a lot of head-scratching.

A Readme file on the XP installation CD. Have you read it?

Run Older Applications On XP

It is universally recognized that XP Home Edition is, in most ways, a vast improvement on its predecessors. This is due to the fact that its architecture is based on NT, the professional version of Windows. However, NT was not designed for the home environment and has never been suitable for certain applications, games being just one example.

With XP, Microsoft have attempted to take the best features from its home environment and professional systems, and combine them into one "super" system.

Unfortunately, it has to be said that they haven't got it quite right yet, and one example of this is the fact that some applications that worked fine on the previous versions will not do so on XP.

Microsoft have recognized this problem, and to help alleviate it have included a Program Compatibility Wizard with XP. The application works by attempting to create the Windows environment in which a particular program will work (Windows 95, 98, ME, NT 4.0 or 2000). Use it as follows:

If applications which worked with your previous version of Windows refuse to do so with XP, don't chuck them out before trying XP's Program Compatibility Wizard.

Once the Wizard has successfully setup a program, the settings will be retained. Every time the program is run, the settings will be applied.

1 Right-click the program, select Properties and then click the Compatibility tab. Select the required operating system

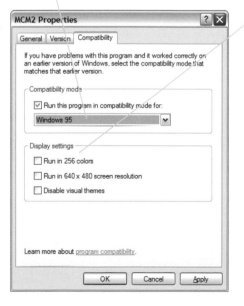

2 Choose any display setting restrictions you may need and then click Apply

3 Click Next. This will test the settings by running the program

4 If it works, tick "Yes, set this program to always use these compatibility settings"

Manage Your Drives With XP

You may find that the Disk Management option is not available from Computer Management. In this case, go back to the Control Panel and click Performance. Then, from the File menu, click Add/Remove Snap-in. In the next dialog box, click Add, in the next select Disk Management, and Add. Then select This Computer in the final dialog box. Go back to Computer Management and Disk Management will now be available.

Disk management with XP Home is basically the process whereby hard drives can be formatted and split into partitions which appear to the system as individual drives. This is a complicated issue which is beyond the scope of this book to adequately address, and should only be attempted by users who know what they are doing.

The ability to do this is not specific to XP; users of ME and earlier versions of Windows can also carry out disk management. The difference with XP is that it is now possible to do it via a Windows interface rather than a DOS interface. This makes it a much more intuitive procedure.

Access XP's disk management utility as described below:

1 Go to Start, Control Panel, Administrative Tools. Click Computer Management and then click Disk Management

You will find that many disk management options are not actually available with the Home edition of XP. To make full use of Disk Management, you will need to run XP Professional.

This utility is not for beginners. Improper use can wipe your drives clean and render your system unusable.

2 The right-hand window shows the drives and partitions installed on the PC

3 Right-clicking a drive shows what options are available

Shortcuts

One of the best ways to increase the efficiency with which a computer is used is by means of shortcuts. The following pages show how to create some useful ones.

Covers

Chapter Nine

Switch Users Quickly

With its Switch User facility, XP makes it easy to switch between users without having to restart the PC and select the desired account from the logon screen. All that's needed is to click the Start button and then the Log Off button.

Click the Switch User button to switch users without restarting the PC

There is, however, an even quicker way of doing it. Try the following:

Only users who are logged on will be seen in the Task Manager User window.

Open the Task Manager by pressing CTRL+ALT+DEL

2 Click the Users tab

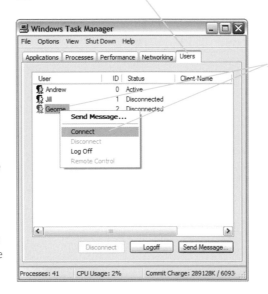

3 Right-click the user you want to switch to and click Connect

From the Users dialog box in the Task Manager, you can also send messages to other users. Just click the Send Message button to open a message box. Type your message and then click OK.

4 The user's Desktop will appear immediately

Note that this tip will only work with users that are actually logged on.

Quickly Switch Between Applications

ALT+TAB Combination

One of the most useful keyboard shortcuts built into all versions of Windows is the ALT+TAB combination.

Holding the ALT key down while pressing the TAB key brings up a menu box showing all your open programs. Tapping the Tab key scrolls through the list, and when it reaches the one you want to open, releasing the ALT key maximizes the program.

This nifty little utility can be extremely useful when you are running a full-screen application, such as a game that obscures the Taskbar.

Task Manager

The Task Manager provides a similar feature.

If you are running a full-screen application that hides the Taskbar, use the ALT+TAB combination or the Task Manager to gain access to your other open programs.

You can also use the tips on this page when you land on a website that opens a full-screen page allowing you no way out.

Note that websites will not be able to do this if you have installed Service Pack 2.

1 Open the Task Manager (CTRL+ALT+DEL) and click the Applications tab

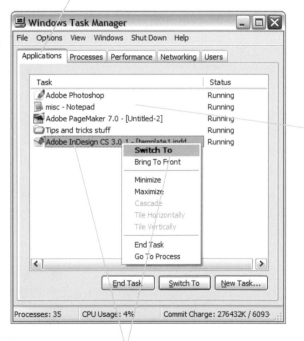

2 Here you will see all the programs running on the PC

3 Right-click the one you want and click Switch To

Add Pop-Up Menus to the Taskbar

This is a simple way of creating useful shortcuts to your favorite applications or files.
Do it as follows:

Good organization is a major factor when it comes to getting a job done quickly and efficiently; this applies to any task. If you have to constantly hunt for your tools, it's surprising how much time will be wasted. The tip on this page will enable you to get a job done on your computer with the minimum of fuss.

I Create a folder on the Desktop and give it a suitable name. Then create shortcuts to all the desired programs in the folder

2 Right-click the Taskbar and select New Toolbar

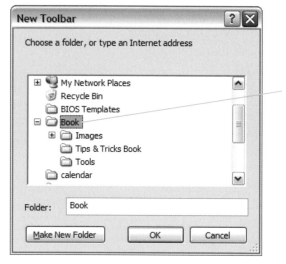

3 Select your shortcut folder and click OK

In the example opposite, we see a pop-up menu containing all the tools used by the author when writing this book.

This menu was accessed constantly and proved to be extremely useful.

Try doing the same with your favorite applications.

4 Now you will see your folder on the Taskbar. Click the chevrons to open a pop-up menu

Create Hotkey Shortcuts

There will be occasions when you want to open a program but don't wish to close the current window so that you can get to it.

You could always click the Show Desktop icon on the Taskbar but you've still got to navigate your way to wherever the program or file is located.

A quicker alternative that doesn't involve using the mouse is described below:

You can create a lot of shortcuts in this way, so many in fact, that you might well have difficulty in remembering them all. Write them down on a piece of paper and stick it on the wall near the monitor.

1 Create a Desktop shortcut to the program by right-clicking it and selecting Send To, Desktop (create shortcut)

2 Right-click the shortcut and select Properties. The following dialog box will open

You can use the tip on this page to open your favorite websites with a single combination keystroke. Simply right-click a web page and select Create Shortcut. A shortcut will be created on the Desktop. Follow steps 2 to 4 to assign a shortcut key to it.

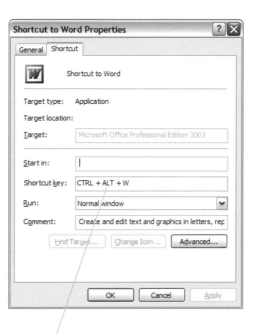

3 Click in the Shortcut key box (this will be reading None)

4 Now simply hit the key you wish to use as the shortcut key – (W) in the example opposite

5 The Shortcut key box will now read CTRL+ALT+W

6 Click OK, and from now on you can open the application by pressing CTRL+ALT+W

Use the Windows Logo Key

All standard keyboards have two Windows logo's keys. These are situated on either side of the space bar and have a logo of a flying window printed on them.

Windows Logo Keys

With these keys you can quickly open a number of applications on your computer.

Refer to the following table:

Key	Action
Windows key	Open the Start Menu
Windows key+D	Minimize or restore all windows
Windows key+E	Open My Computer
Windows key+F	Open Windows search utility
Windows key+R	Open Run dialog box
Windows key+BREAK	Open System Properties dialog box
Windows key+SHIFT+M	Undo minimize all windows
Windows key+U	Open Utility Manager
Windows key+L	Lock Computer
Windows key+F1	Open Windows Help menu

Document1 - Microso

File   Edit   View   Insert

New...
Open...
Close
Save
Save As...
Save as Web Page...
File Search...

How to Do a Quick Keyword Search

The ability to carry out almost instantaneous searches is an extremely useful and often overlooked feature of computers.

By using the Windows Search application, it is possible to carry out an entire search of a computer's contents for literally anything. To do this though, it is necessary to set up various search parameters, and thus it cannot really be described as quick.

This tip can be used with Windows text applications such as Notepad and WordPad. It can also be very useful when carrying out searches on the Internet. Some web pages can be extremely long, and if you are looking for a particular topic and find yourself wading through reams of unrelated stuff, using Ctrl+F can be a real time-saver.

However, Windows does provide another, more basic, search tool which can be used for carrying out quick searches in text-based applications, such as word-processors and web pages.

Let's say, for example, that you have opened a lengthy web page and are looking for all instances of a specific word, but have neither the time or inclination to read through the whole page.

What you need to do is press Ctrl+F on your keyboard; this will open the Find dialog box, as shown below:

1 Type the word you wish to find in the Find what box and click the Find Next button

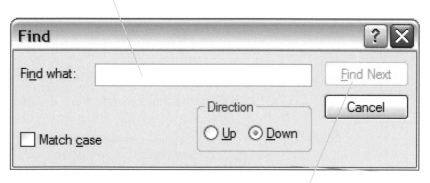

2 To find further instances, click the Find Next button again

3 By selecting Up or Down, you can direct the search

This tip will work in all Windows text applications and some non-Windows applications.

Easy Email

With this tip, you can create instant links to your favorite contacts and place them all in a folder on the Desktop. Alternatively, you can use the folder to create a Taskbar pop-up menu as described on page 118.

This is a handy tip for those of you who do a lot of emailing. Instead of starting Outlook Express each time you want to send a message to someone, and then clicking the Create Mail button on the menu bar, you can achieve the same thing from the Desktop with one click. Here's how to do it:

Right-click the Desktop and select New, Shortcut. You will see the following dialog box:

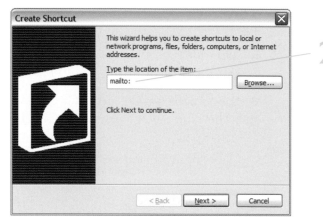

2 In the box type mailto: Then click Next. Give it a suitable name and then click Finish

You can create pre-addressed message boxes to anyone you like, simply by entering their email address after "mailto:".

You will now see a new Outlook Express icon on the Desktop. Click it and an open email message window will appear.

As a refinement of this tip, you can have the message window open with the address already filled in. To do this all you have to do is enter the required email address immediately after "mailto:" in step 2. For example, if you enter "mailto:stuart.yarnold@ntl.com" your email will open with this address in the To box. Then type in your message and hit Send.

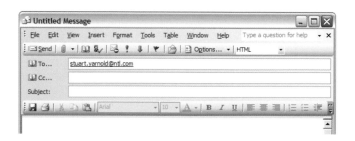

One-Click Shutdown/Restart Icons

To shutdown your computer with XP you need to click Start, Turn Off Computer and then Shutdown – 3 clicks in total. It is possible to do it with just one click, however.

Having created your Restart and Shutdown icons, you will probably want to make them look a bit more interesting. Do the following:

1) Right-click the icon

2) Click the Shortcut tab and then click Change Icon

3) In the Change Icon dialog box, click OK

4) Choose the new icon, click OK and OK again

Right-click the Desktop and select New, Shortcut. You will see the following dialog box:

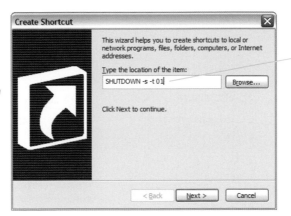

2 In the box type SHUTDOWN -s -t 01 and click Next

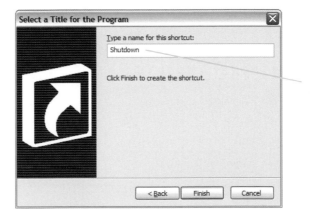

3 Give the short-cut a suitable name such as "Shutdown" and then click Finish

Shutdown

You will now see the Shutdown icon on the Desktop. This can be left where it is or dragged to the Taskbar.

To create a Restart icon, instead of typing SHUTDOWN -s -t 01 in Step 2, type SHUTDOWN -r -t 01

Windows Keyboard Shortcuts

In certain situations, using the keyboard can be a much easier way of controlling a computer. A typical example is using a Notebook while on a train or a plane. The following is a selection of useful keyboard shortcuts:

The following are some useful application-specific shortcuts that work with most Microsoft Office and other Windows applications:

1) CTRL+O – opens a document from within an application

2) CTRL+N – opens a new document

3) CTRL+S – saves work in progress and is a particularly useful shortcut

A mouse-free method for shutting down Windows XP is to tap the Windows key (or press CTRL+ESC), then press U to select "Turn Off Computer" from the menu. From there, type S to put the computer into Standby mode, U to turn it off, or R to restart Windows.

Key	Action
CTRL+C	Copy
CTRL+X	Cut
CTRL+V	Paste
CTRL+Z	Undo
DELETE	Delete
SHIFT+DELETE	Delete an item permanently
CTRL while dragging	Copy the selected item
CTR+SHIFT while dragging	Create a shortcut to the selected item
F2	Rename the selected item
CTRL+A	Select all
F3	Search for a file or toolbar
ALT+ENTER	View the properties for the selected item
ALT+F4	Close the active item or program
ALT+SPACEBAR	Open the shortcut menu for the active window
CTRL+F4	Close the active document
ALT+TAB	Switch between the open items
ALT+ESC	Cycle through items in the order opened
F6	Cycle through screen elements
F4	Display the address bar list
SHIFT+F10	Display the selected item's shortcut menu
CTRL+ESC	Display the Start menu
F10	Activate the menu bar in the active program
RIGHT ARROW	Open the next menu to the right
LEFT ARROW	Open the next menu to the left
F5	Update (refresh) the active window
BACKSPACE	View the folder one level up
ESC	Cancel the current task

The Internet

There is an almost endless amount of tips and tricks to help get the best out of the Internet and Internet Explorer. These include increasing the reliability of connections, increasing browsing speed and how to prevent disrupted downloads.

Covers

Chapter Ten

Minimize Interrupted Downloads

Download managers can be configured to begin a download at a specified time. They will automatically make the Internet connection using your Dial-up Network settings, begin the download, and when it is completed, break the connection. If your connection should fail during the download for some reason, they will redial and then resume the download.

Anyone who downloads data from the Internet will, at one time or another, experience the frustration of an unexpected disruption to their download. This can be a result of the modem going offline for some reason or the Internet Service Provider (ISP) breaking the connection (many ISPs will deliberately sever the connection after a set period).

Unfortunately, Internet Explorer doesn't have the ability to resume interrupted downloads, and so you then have to start the process all over again. This is not too bad if it is a small download, but if you are downloading a large program you could have wasted several hours.

While there are things you can do to optimize your connection and thus minimize the risk of a broken connection (discussed on pages 128–129), there is no way to eliminate this problem completely. However, there is a way to minimize its effects and this comes in the form of what's known as a "download manager."

These are programs which monitor a download, and if it is interrupted for whatever reason, will resume it from the point at which the download stopped. This means you don't have to start again from the beginning. They also offer other useful features such as increased download speeds, automatic scheduling, automatic redial and easy-to-see details regarding file size, download time and so on. Various options from a download manager called "Getright" are shown below.

Download managers can often increase the download speed of a file. They do this by building a list of "mirror sites," all of which have the file available for download. During the download, the program will automatically switch between the mirror sites to find the one offering the best download conditions.

There are various programs of this type on the market, two of the best being GetRight and Gozilla. Both of these are easily obtainable from computer magazine cover CDs. You can also download them from the manufacturers' websites. To download GetRight, go to: www.getright.com. Gozilla is available at: www.gozilla.com.

Getright is a shareware application which means you don't have to pay for it as long as you are prepared to put up with various advertisements and reminders. Gozilla is offered on a thirty day trial basis, after which you must pay for it.

The screenshot below is taken from GetRight and shows a download in progress. Various information is available from this window.

In terms of performance and features, there is little to choose between Getright and Gozilla. However, Getright is free (as long as you don't mind nag screens), whereas Gozilla is not. For this reason, Getright is the recommended program.

Name of the file being downloaded

Progress indicator

The size of the file

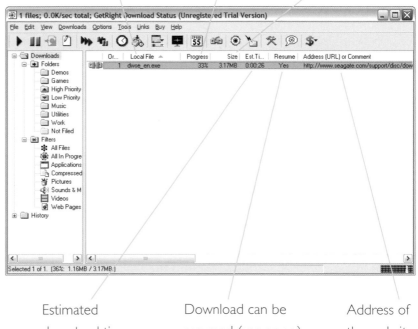

Estimated download time

Download can be resumed (yes or no)

Address of the website

Keep Your Dial-Up Connection Alive

You lose your connection at periodic intervals for no apparent reason. There are several causes of this problem.

Idle Disconnect

If your connection keeps failing after exactly the same period, do the following:

Idle Disconnect is a safety feature which automatically disconnects the modem after a specified period. Its purpose is to prevent a user from clocking up a huge telephone bill if, for some reason, the user forgets to log off.

1 Go to Start, Control Panel, Phone and Modem Options. Click the Modems tab, highlight and right-click your modem. From the right-click menu click Properties. In the next dialog box, click the Advanced tab and then click Change Default Preferences

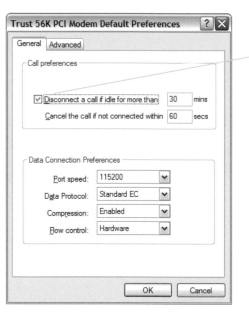

2 Untick the "Disconnect a call if idle for more than" box

Ensure that memory phones and faxes are disconnected from the line. Some of these have small rechargeable capacitors which maintain the memory of the device. These capacitors recharge from the phone line periodically, and in some cases can disconnect the modem.

Programs/Devices Which Activate Suddenly

Applications such as Advanced Power Management, and screensavers can break your connection when they "kick in." Try disabling them.

Remove any other devices connected to the telephone line that might be causing interference, such as phones, answering machines and fax machines. These can all cause a connection to be dropped.

Call waiting is a method of alerting someone who's using a phone that someone else is trying to ring them; this is indicated by a beep. If the phone line is being used for Internet access, this beep can break the connection, and even if it doesn't, will cause the connection to pause or slow down for a short period.

You can eliminate this by disabling Call Waiting as described opposite. However, then you won't know when someone is trying to contact you. If you need to know this, there are several options available:

1) You can buy a Call Waiting modem which lets you know if there's an incoming call and provides answering options

2) Get a second phone line

3) Upgrade your connection to broadband

4) Try an Internet Call Waiting Service

Call Waiting

If this feature is enabled, it can break your Internet connection when another call comes in. Disable it as follows:

Open Phone and Modem Options in the Control Panel. Highlight the connection and then click Edit

Tick "To disable call waiting, dial". In the box, select *70

Transmit/Receive Buffers

The COM port transmit/receive buffers are used to regulate the flow of data between the modem and PC. If they are set too high, connection problems can result. Try resetting them as follows:

Go to Control Panel, Phone and Modem Options. Click the modem and click Properties. Then click the Advanced tab and Advanced Port Settings (see bottom margin note)

The Advanced Port Settings dialog box may not be available with certain modems.

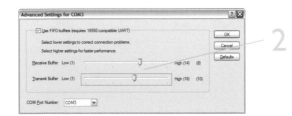

Reduce the size of the buffers by dragging the sliders to the left

The best setting will be a trade-off between speed and performance.

Speed Up Your Connection

There are three main causes of slow dial-up connections:

- A noisy telephone line
- An incorrectly configured modem
- The ISP

Slow connections can also be caused by congested networks. At certain times (evenings and weekends), many more people will be online; bear this in mind.

Check them out in the order above.

Swift and reliable network access depends on many factors, and the one most commonly overlooked is the telephone line itself. An obvious indicator of problems in this area is line static. Another is if your connection speed is significantly less than it should be. If you sometimes hear crackling when you use the phone, there is a bad connection on the circuit. Contact the phone company and get them to fix it. You can also ask them to increase the "gain" on the line. This basically means the level of signal amplification, and a higher level can make a significant difference.

Next, check that your modem is set up correctly.

1 Go to Start, Control Panel, Phone and Modem Options

2 Click the Modems tab

To perform at its best, a modem must be using the driver designed for it. Other drivers, such as XP's generic "Standard" modem driver, may work but they won't allow the modem to function optimally.

3 Here you will see details of the installed driver. If it is the wrong one, select it and click Remove. Then install the correct one by clicking Add

Note that while a modem may well work with an incorrect driver, it won't perform optimally; you must use the one supplied.

Next, check that the modem is operating at its maximum speed. Do this as follows:

If your system is in an unstable condition, you could experience problems when surfing the net. Try rebooting the PC – this will clear the system's memory, and also close or reset any service or application which might be causing problems.

If your web browsing is persistently slow, you may need more RAM in your system.

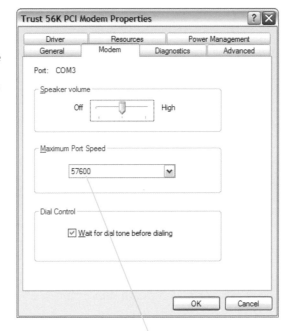

Go to Start, Control Panel and Phone and Modem Options. Click the Modems tab and then click Properties

2 Click the Modem tab and check that the Maximum Port Speed is set to the modem's maximum connection speed

If your modem is an older model, it could well benefit from an upgrade. Visit the manufacturer's website, and you should find both a driver and firmware upgrade available for free download. The firmware upgrade will reprogram your modem and allow it to take advantage of the latest V.92 modem technology.

If you're still suffering from slow connections, check out your ISP. The easiest way to do this is to try another one – there's no shortage of them about. There's nothing to stop you having two or more accounts; if you have problems with one, just switch to another.

Be wary of low-cost ISPs. To make it pay, they are quite likely to allot each user a narrower bandwidth. This will translate into slower connection speeds.

Finally, consider signing up for a broadband connection. This will give you all the speed you want, plus the added benefit of an "always-on" connection. A further advantage is that your telephone won't be tied up by the connection.

Speed Up Your Browser

Your system is quite likely to be loaded with malware if you are in the habit of doing any of the following:

1) Downloading Shareware and Freeware applications

2) Downloading files from peer-to-peer networks such as Kazaa and File Donkey

Malware

Currently, one of the main causes of slow browsing speeds is the presence of numerous instances of spyware and adware programs on a system.

These applications exist to regale you with advertisments and use your Internet connection to do so. The more you have on your system (it's not uncommon for PCs to have dozens of these programs), the slower your browser will be.

Brower Hijackers

Even worse than spyware and adware, is the plague of browser hijackers currently running amok on the Internet. These pernicious programs can take over your browser completely and persistently redirect your searches to pay-per-click search engines.

They can also be the cause of the following:

- A new toolbar suddenly appears in your browser
- Internet Explorer slows to a crawl
- All web searches are redirected to other sites – you have no control over your browser
- Your homepage is reset to a different site and all attempts to remove it are blocked
- You get a continuous assault of porn pop-up windows
- Porn and advertising sites are bookmarked in Internet Favorites
- A marked decrease in overall PC performance

Browser hijackers get onto a system by exploiting security loopholes in Internet Explorer. While it won't get rid of hijackers already on a system, installing XP Service Pack 2 will prevent any more.

Apart from their unsavory aspects, the worst effect of these hijackers is the way they reduce your browser to a crawl. They can also severely affect the stability and performance of the computer itself.

There are several applications on the market which will rid a system of most malware and hijackers – see pages 25–26. However, many malware/hijacking programs are extremely devious and so can be very hard to detect. They can be even harder to remove (the "CoolWebSearch" hijacker, for example, installs multiple instances of itself in the system's Registry under different names). In worst case scenarios, a clean reinstallation of XP will be the only way to purge a system completely.

Browser Cache (Temporary Internet Files folder)

If you are having problems with the way some websites load, or if the web seems unusually slow, the problem may be with the browser cache. This is a folder on your computer where the browser saves copies of visited web pages. It does this so that if you visit the page again it will load faster. In time this folder will fill up with literally thousands of files; a potential consequence of which is that rather than speeding up browsing, as it is intended to do, it will actually slow it down. To prevent this, periodically clear out the cache.

There is a setting in Internet Options that when enabled, will automatically clear the browser cache when it is shut down.

You can access this by opening Internet Options and clicking the Advanced tab. Scroll down until you see the "Empty Temporary Internet Files Folder when browser is closed" checkbox.

Go to Start, Control Panel and open Internet Options. Under Temporary Internet Files, click Delete files

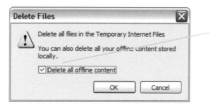

Tick the Delete all offline content box and then click OK

Disable Graphics in Internet Explorer

Graphics are the slowest-loading element of a web page, and for this reason, a site which contains many graphics can take a long time to open. Plain text, however, is the quickest element; if this is the type of content you wish to access, do the following:

The issue of graphics is one of the main considerations when it comes to website design. This is worth remembering in case you should ever decide to build a site or homepage of your own.

A well-designed site will keep graphic content to the minimum, as most people simply click past a slow-loading page. Take a look at the sites of major corporations: the vast majority of them have few, if any, advertising banners, and links will be text-based rather than graphic.

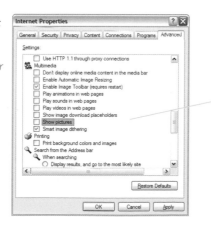

Go to the Control Panel and open Internet Options. Then click the Advanced tab

Scroll down and you will see options to disable animations, sound, videos and images. Disabling these will speed up web page access times significantly

How to Repair Internet Explorer

Another way of repairing Internet Explorer is to download it from the Microsoft website. Go to: www.microsoft.com/windows/ie/downloads/critical/ie6sp1/default.asp.

However, if you are on a dial-up connection this is perhaps not so feasible, as the download will be approximately 25 MB.

Alternatively, you can order it from Microsoft on a CD, providing you live in the USA or Canada.

For those of you with a broadband connection, however, downloading it should present no problem.

If you do have a broadband connection and your current version of Internet Explorer is not the latest, then it makes sense to download the latest version rather than repairing it as described on this page.

If you have Windows XP Service Pack 2 installed on your system then you already have the latest version of Internet Explorer – this is integrated into SP2.

To find out which version of Internet Explorer you are currently using, open it, and from the Help menu, click About Internet Explorer.

Internet Explorer is a highly complex piece of software, and as with XP itself can, over time, become corrupted to the extent that it no longer works properly, or little niggles and errors develop.

With most applications, the solution to this problem is to simply reinstall the program. However, there is no obvious way of doing this with Internet Explorer, other than to reinstall XP itself.

There is a way to do it though, and this is described below:

1   Place the XP installation disk in the CD drive

2   Go to Start and click Search. Under "What do you want to search for" click All files and folders

3   In the top box type ie.inf

4   Select More Advanced Options and place a check mark beside the Search Hidden Files and Folders option

5   Ensure that the Search System Folders and Search Sub folders boxes are also checked

6   In the Look In drop-down box, select the letter of the hard drive that contains the Windows folder (usually C). Then click Search

7   When you see the ie.inf file in the search results, right-click it and then click Install

8   Internet Explorer will now be reinstalled from the XP CD

When the file transfer is complete, reboot the computer.

Set Your Own Homepage

A common trick employed by many Internet Service Providers is to automatically set Internet Explorer's start page to their own site when their software is installed. By using the tip on this page, you will be able to restore your preferred start page.

When you start Internet Explorer, perhaps not surprisingly, it immediately heads for Microsoft's MSN search engine. It does this because during the XP installation procedure, the Microsoft site is installed as the default startup web page. If you seldom or never visit this particular site, it can be a pain. It would be much more practical if Internet Explorer took you straight to a site that you do visit frequently. For example, if you use the Internet to keep track of your share prices, as many do, you could go directly to the website that you use for this purpose.

To configure Internet Explorer to do this, do the following:

1 Go to Start, Control Panel, Internet Options. In the dialog box that opens, select the General tab

If you wish to use a specific page within a site as the start page but aren't sure of what URL to enter, do the following:

Logon, open the desired page in your browser, and in the address bar at the top you will see the page's URL. Simply copy/paste it to the address box in step 2 opposite.

2 Highlight the current entry in the Address box (the Microsoft site), and then type in the address of your favored site.

3 Click Apply

Using the above example, from now on, each time you start Internet Explorer it will automatically go to the BBC website at: www.bbc.com.

How to Back Up Your Favorites

Another method of backing up your Favorites is to locate the Favorites folder and simply copy it to a backup location or drive. You will find it in the Documents and Settings folder. Open this and then open the relevant user folder. This is where the Favorites folder resides.

Over time, many people build up a huge list of carefully categorized Favorite links to sites they frequently access. Losing the list can be nothing short of a minor disaster.

If you have such a list and don't relish the prospect of building it up again, back it up as follows:

1 From Internet Explorer's File menu, select Import and Export. This opens the Import and Export wizard

2 Select Export Favorites

3 Select the folder to be backed up

4 Browse to the backup folder and click Next. In the final dialog box, click Finish

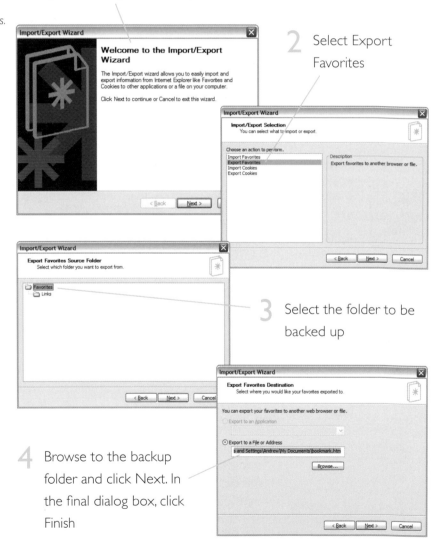

File-Sharing

For those of you not yet in the know, file-sharing is one of the Internet's fastest growing applications. It makes use of specialized peer-to-peer networks and software, which allow computer users to connect directly to the computers of other users in the same network. The purpose of it all lies in the name – file sharing, which really says it all. Each user can designate certain files on their PC which they are willing to share.

To take part in this activity, you need a file-sharing program. These are available for free on the Internet and there are literally dozens of them (go to www.download.com and enter file-sharing in the search box).

Simply download and install the program, designate which files you want to share with other users, and you're all set to go. Good examples of this type of application are Winmx (www.winmx.com), Kazaa (www.kazaa.com) and Emule (www.emule-project.net).

Of all the file-sharing programs, Emule (shown below) is considered to be the best. It is also free of all adware and spyware, something that cannot be said for most of them.

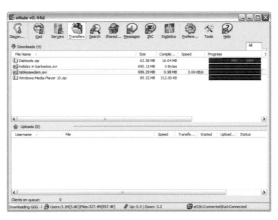

When using these programs, there are two things to be aware of: Firstly, while the use of the program is legal, the downloading of copyrighted material is most definitely not.

Secondly, many of these programs will also install a lot of malware on your PC. Be wary of this.

Save Your Files On the Internet

XP provides a feature that not many people are aware of and which can be very useful. This is its Web Publishing utility, which allows users to save files on the Internet.

In effect, this utility provides an online hard drive, although, it must be said, not a very large one – each user is limited to 25 MB of storage space. However, if you use it to store text documents, which are very small in size, it can be very useful indeed.

1 Open the folder containing the file to be saved, select the file, and on the left-hand side under File and Folder Tasks, click Publish this file to the Web

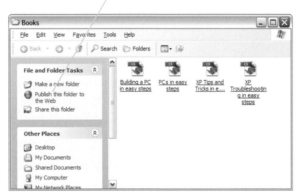

2 The Web Publishing Wizard will open

If you decide to set up an online drive with the Web Publishing utility, you will need a MSN, Hotmail or Passport email address. If you haven't got one, then you'll also have to go through the procedure of setting one up.

3 Follow the prompts, and very soon your files will be saved in your very own piece of Cyberspace

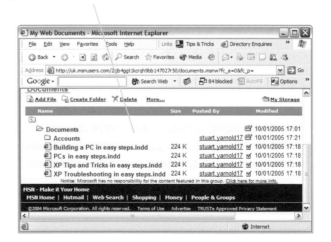

Microsoft are not the only company who offer free web storage space. There are, in fact, any number of websites that you can visit to create an account, which can then be used to upload and download files as desired.

Some examples are:

- *www.filesanywhere.com*
- *www.mydocsonline.com*
- *www.myspace.com*

The only caveat with this is that before you can save your files online, you will need to have a MSN, Hotmail or Passport email address. If you haven't, you'll need to set up an account.

How to Date a Web Page

No, this isn't some sort of strange perversion; it's actually a tip that will be extremely useful to many people.

The Internet is a mine of information concerning just about every subject known to man. However, just as books eventually become dated unless periodically revised, so do all the millions of web pages.

It's a bit of a pain to have to type this into your browser every time you want to check a page. A good idea is to type it into a Notepad document and then drag the document to the Links toolbar on your browser. Then you can just open the Notepad document and copy/paste the command into your browser as and when needed.

You can find out instantly how current the contents of any book are simply by looking at the date of publication inside the front cover. Very few websites, though, offer any guide in this respect, and so the surfer may well be reading content that is, in fact, years out of date and will, in many cases, be completely useless.

However, there is a way to determine how old a web page is and you can do it as follows:

1   Open the relevant page in your browser and in the address box type the following: javascript:alert(document.lastModified)

This tip has only been tested with Internet Explorer. It may not work with other browsers, such as Firefox and Opera.

2   Press Go or Enter on the keyboard and a pop-up will appear telling you the time and date the page was last modified

Power Surfing

This is a very simple yet extremely effective tip for those of you who like to surf the web using search engines as a starting point.

When doing this, most people simply click on a link that interests them, and when finished with it use the back button to return to the search engine. This is OK, but does involve using the back and forward buttons a lot.

Try doing it this way:

Instead of opening one browser window, open two. Then right-click on the Taskbar and choose "Tile Windows Vertically." Now adjust the size of the two browser windows so that the one on the left is about three inches wide and the other fills the rest of the screen. This is demonstrated below.

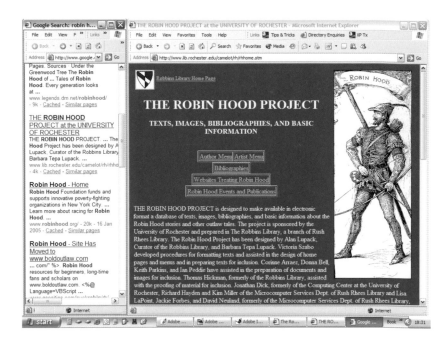

Open the search engine in the smaller window and then simply drag a link that interests you into the bigger one. Now you can browse whilst having your list of links in view at all times. To open a new link (or reopen one) just drag it into the main window. No more constantly hitting the Back and Forward buttons.

Use All Your Download Bandwidth

This tip will allow you to have up to ten different downloads running simultaneously. By doing this you will be utilizing the large bandwidth offered by broadband much more efficiently.

By default, the maximum number of simultaneous downloads possible with Internet Explorer 6 is two. The reason for this dates back to the early days of the Internet when connections were of the slow dial-up type. For users of high-speed broadband, this two-connection limit has become restrictive as it doesn't allow the user to fully utilize the available bandwidth offered by broadband.

However, courtesy of a simple Registry tweak, it is possible to configure Internet Explorer to allow up to ten simultaneous downloads. Do it as described below:

1 Open the Registry Editor and locate the following key: HKEY_CURRENT_USER\Software\Microsoft\Windows\ CurrentVersion\Internet Settings

Users of dial-up connections will gain no benefit from doing this as they do not have enough bandwidth.

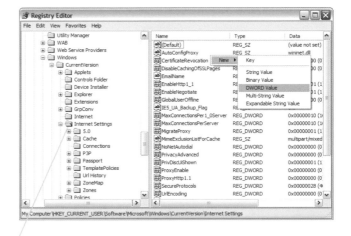

2 Click the Internet Settings folder

3 Right-click in the right-hand window, create a New DWORD value and name it: MaxConnectionsPer1_0Server. Double-click this and set a value of 10

4 In the same window, create another DWORD value and name it: MaxConnectionsPerServer. Give this a value of 10 as well. Exit the Registry and restart XP for the change to take effect

How to Change Internet Explorer's Default Search Engine

This is a much requested tip as many people are not that keen on the MSN search engine that is the default Internet Explorer search engine. You can change this to the search engine of your own choice (Google in this example), as follows:

You can use this tip to specify any search engine as Internet Explorer's default search engine. All you have to do is enter its address in step 2 and step 4.

1 Open the Registry Editor and locate the following key: HKEY_CURRENT_USER\Software\Microsoft\Internet Explorer\ Main

2 Click the Main folder and in the right-hand window locate the Search Page entry. Double-click this and change the value data to: http://www.google.com

3 Locate the following key: HKEY_LOCAL_MACHINE\Software\Microsoft\Internet Explorer\ Search

4 Click the Search folder and in the right-hand window locate the SearchAssistant entry. Double-click this and change the value data to: http://www.google.com/ie. Close the Registry Editor

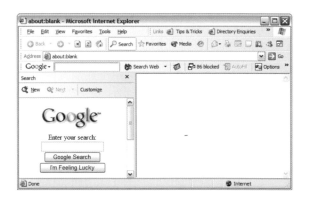

5 To use a different search engine, simply substitute its address for www.google. com

Click the Search button in Internet Explorer and it will now open with Google.

Stop Desktop Spam Messages

A problem that many users new to XP soon encounter, particularly if they have a broadband connection, is unsolicited spam messages periodically popping up on the Desktop.

The Messenger Service is intended for use by system administrators to notify Windows users about their networks. However, many advertisers are misusing this service to send spam.

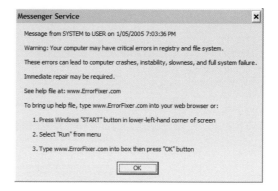

Although the name is similar, XP's Messenger Service is not related to Windows Messenger. Disabling Windows Messenger will not prevent Messenger Service spam being downloaded to your computer.

This Service provides no useful purpose to users and so can be safely disabled.

These messages are transmitted via XP's Messenger Service and to get rid of them permanently, you need to disable the Messenger Service. Do it as follows:

Go to Start, Control Panel, Administrative Tools. Click Services. Locate the Messenger Service and double-click it

Installing XP Service Pack 2 will automatically disable XP's Messenger Service.

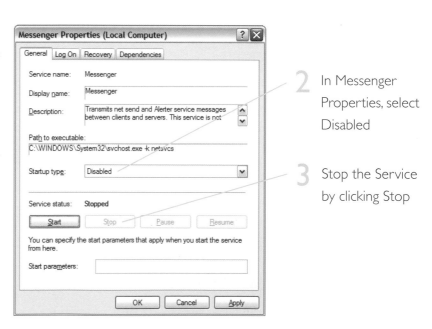

2 In Messenger Properties, select Disabled

3 Stop the Service by clicking Stop

Miscellaneous Internet Explorer Tips

Quick Printing

Rather than print out an entire page when all you want is a paragraph, do the following:

You can also choose to print only the text and graphics, and not the background colors and images of a web page. Select Internet Options from the Tools menu and go to the Advanced tab. Scroll down to Printing and uncheck Print background colors and images. Click Apply and then OK.

1 Highlight the desired text, right-click and select Print

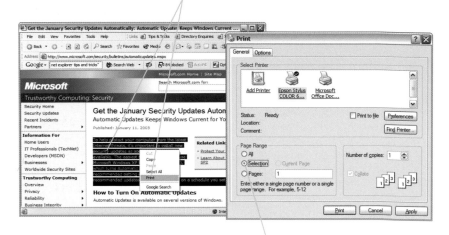

2 In the printer software, choose Selection. Only the selected text will be printed

Stop the Kids Downloading

This is easy.

Have you ever visited a site where the right-click menu has been disabled, thus preventing you from downloading something from the page. The next time you do, try pressing CTRL+N. This will open the page in a new window in which the right-click menu will sometimes work.

1 Go to Internet Options in the Control Panel. Click the Security tab, press the Custom Level button and scroll down to the Downloads section

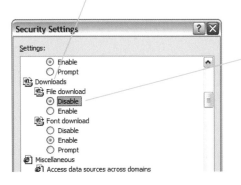

2 Select the Disable button. Now you needn't worry about what the little horrors are up to

Open a Link in a Separate Window

This is a simple tip that allows you to open a link while keeping the current page open. In some situations this can be useful as it allows you to switch quickly between the two pages.

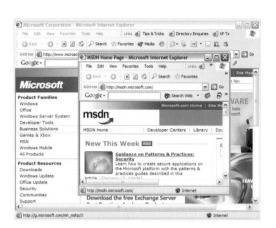

All you have to do is hold the Shift key down as you click the link. The new page will then open in a new Internet Explorer window.

Quick Search From Internet Explorer's Address Bar

Rather than opening up a search engine, try the following:

In the address bar type ?, Go or Find, followed by the keyword. Then press Enter

Kill the Pop-Up Messages

If used for the right purpose, such as displaying useful information, pop-up windows are an acceptable part of browsing the Internet. Unfortunately, they are all too often used to display irritating advertisments and other such stuff. The solution to this problem is to use a pop-up blocker.

As with everything else, some pop-up blockers are better than others. The Google and SP2 blockers mentioned on this page block all pop-ups, useful or otherwise. They are, however, free.

You can also get "intelligent" blockers which can differentiate between useful windows and pop-up advertisments. You will need to pay for these though.

One that the author recommends comes with the Google Toolbar (a useful browser add-on in itself). You can download this from: http://toolbar.google.com.

Toggle the Google pop-up blocker on and off

Alternatively, install XP Service Pack 2. This adds a pop-up blocker to Internet Explorer.

Stop Script Debugging Error Messages

A problem that can occur when browsing the Internet with Internet Explorer is the sudden appearance of "Script Debug" error messages. These usually say something like "Script error at line 01. Do you wish to debug?" These messages can be persistent and extremely irritating.

Internet Explorer's Script Debugging utility is a troubleshooting tool designed for website developers. For the average user it serves no purpose at all. Although it is disabled by default, some applications can enable it. If these messages suddenly start appearing, disable Script Debugging as described opposite.

Get rid of them as follows:

1 Go to Start, Control Panel, Internet Options. Click the Advanced tab

2 Scroll down to Disable Script Debugging and tick the box

3 In the same window, untick the "Display a notification about every script error" box

Internet Explorer Key Shortcuts

The following table shows some useful Internet Explorer keyboard shortcuts.

Many Internet Explorer operations are actually quicker using the keyboard. For example, the Backspace key is much easier to use than the Back button. Also, try using the Up and Down Arrow keys to scroll through pages. The Home and End keys are other useful keys that take you quickly to the beginning and end of documents.

If you've managed to find one of those sites that open a full-screen page that doesn't give you an escape route, simply hit CTRL+W. This will close the window.

Command	Action
F11	Toggles between full-screen and other views
TAB	Move forward through the items on a Web page, the Address box, or the Links box
SHIFT+TAB	Move through the items on a Web page, the Address box, or the Links box
ALT+HOME	Go to your Home page
ALT+RIGHT ARROW	Go to the next page
ALT+LEFT ARROW	Go to the previous page
SHIFT+F10	Display a shortcut menu for a link
CTRL+TAB or F6	Move forward between frames
UP ARROW	Scroll toward the beginning of a document
DOWN ARROW	Scroll toward the end of a document
PAGE UP	Scroll toward the beginning of a document in larger increments
PAGE DOWN	Scroll toward the end of a document in larger increments
HOME	Move to the beginning of a document
END	Move to the end of a document
CTRL+F	Find on this page
CTRL+R or F5	Refresh the current Web page
ESC	Stop downloading a page
CTRL+O	Go to a new location
CTRL+N	Open a new window
CTRL+W	Close the current window
CTRL+P	Print the current page or active frame
ENTER	Activate a selected link
CTRL+E	Open the Search box
CTRL+I	Open the Favorites box

Some more Internet Explorer keyboard shortcuts:

Type the main part of an address and then press CTRL+ENTER. This will automatically add the www. and .com to complete the address. This only works for addresses ending with .com, however.

Command	Action
ALT+MINUS	Zoom out
ALT+PLUS	Zoom in
ALT+P	Set printing options and print the page
ALT+D	Select the text in the address bar
CTRL+A	Select all the items on the current web page
CTRL+X	Remove selected items and copy them to the clipboard
CTRL+E	Open the search bar
CTRL+B	Open the Organize Favorites dialog box
CTRL+V	Insert the contents of the clipboard
CTRL+CLICK	In the History or Favorites bars, open multiple folders
BACKSPACE	Go to the previous page
F4	Display a list of addresses you've typed
CTRL+C	Copy the selected items to the clipboard
ALT+C	Close print preview
CTRL+D	Add the current page to your Favorites
CTRL+ENTER	Add www. to the beginning and .com to the end of the text typed in the address bar
CTRL+RIGHT ARROW	When in the Address bar, move the cursor right to the next logical break in the address
CTRL+LEFT ARROW	When in the Address bar, move the cursor left to the next logical break in the address
ALT+F	Specify how you want frames to print. This option is available only if you are printing a web page that uses frames
CTRL+F5	Refresh the current web page, even if the time stamp for the Web and locally stored versions are the same
CTRL+H	Open the History box

Press CTRL+D to instantly add the current web page to your Favorites folder.

Email

Two of the biggest problems people experience when using email are junk mail and viruses. This chapter shows how to deal with these issues.

There are also tips on how to keep your messages and account settings safe, plus some useful keyboard shortcuts.

Covers

Chapter Eleven

How to Back Up Email Messages

The ability to send and receive email is a very important function of the modern day computer, and just as people often like to keep personal letters, they also like to keep their email. Email is also an important means of business communication and these emails usually need to be kept as records.

Unfortunately, Outlook Express, which is the email program used by most people, does not provide a simple means of creating backup copies of its message folders. There is a way to do it though.

If you wish to change the default folder that Outlook Express uses to store messages, go to Tools, Options, and Maintenance. Click Store Folder and you will see the folder currently being used and its location. By clicking the Change button you can specify a different folder and location.

1 Create a backup folder and give it a suitable name

2 Open Outlook Express and from the Tools menu, click Options. Then click the Maintenance tab

Another, more laborious way to back up your emails is to individually open each message by double-clicking it and then, from the Edit menu, selecting Save As. You can then save it where you like. However, while this will create a copy of your messages, you will not be able to restore them to Outlook Express.

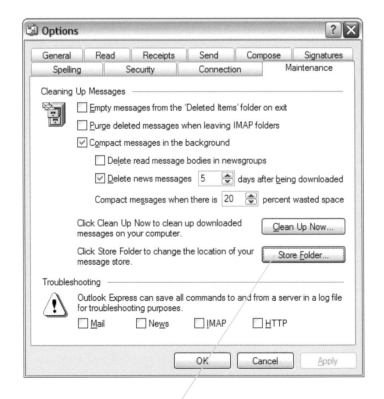

3 Click the Store Folder button

Users of Outlook, a more powerful email program, have an easier way to back up their messages. This is the Import and Export wizard, which is available from the File menu. Using this you can quickly create a copy of your email data.

There is also an automatic backup utility available for download on Microsoft's website (see page 181).

4 The dialog box that opens shows the location of your email files

5 Highlight the address, right-click and click Copy

6 Go to the Start Menu and open the Run box. Right-click in the box and click Paste. Then click OK

7 The email messages folder will now open

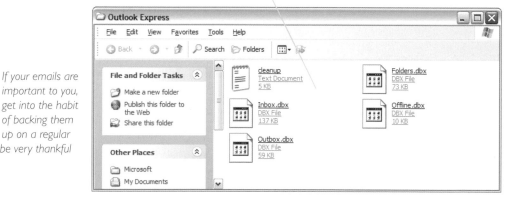

If your emails are important to you, get into the habit of backing them up on a regular basis. You may be very thankful one day.

8 Now all you have to do is copy the contents of the email folder to your backup folder

Should you ever need to restore your email messages, simply reverse the above procedure.

How to Back Up Email Accounts

Unlike email messages, Outlook Express does provide an easy way to back up your account settings.

Do it as follows:

When creating your backup, it is a good idea to store it on a different medium. In the case of email account settings, a floppy disk is ideal. However, floppies do not have a large enough capacity to use as backups for your email messages.

1 Create a backup folder with a suitable name. Open Outlook Express and go to Tools, Accounts. Click the Mail tab

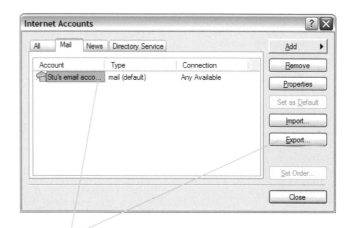

2 Select the account you want to backup. Then click Export

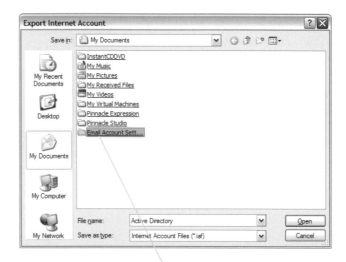

3 Browse to your backup folder, open it and then click Save

How to Back Up the Address Book

Users of Outlook have no obvious way of backing up the address book; this is perhaps because the address book has been largely supplanted by Outlook's "Contacts" utility. Contacts offers many more features and options and can be backed up by going to the File menu and selecting Import and Export.

Many people make very good use of their address book. Not only can they store all their email addresses in it, but also other useful stuff such as addresses, telephone numbers and personal information.

If they should ever lose all this information, which has probably been compiled over a period of years, it could be nothing short of a minor disaster to them.

To guard against this possibility, a backup copy should be made. Fortunately, Outlook Express makes this easy.

1   Open Outlook Express and from the toolbar, click Addresses. This opens the Address Book

2   From the Address Book's File menu, select Export and then click Address Book (WAB)

3   The Save In dialog box will now open. Give the file a name, select a storage location and then click Save

4   To restore your Address Book, repeat steps 1 and 2, only this time, select Import, and browse to wherever your backup is located. Then click Open

How to Open Blocked Attachments in Outlook Express

Be careful when opening attachments. The virus protection feature has been introduced for a good reason, as viruses transmitted via email are nearly always in an attachment to the message.

Before you open any attachment, take a look at its file extension, and if it is of a dangerous type (see pages 156–57), just delete it.

Viruses transmitted by email are almost always contained in an attachment to the email. However, the attachment must be opened by the user before the virus can be released.

To prevent this, Outlook Express 6 (SP1 and SP2) has a virus protection feature that prevents any attachment that it considers unsafe from being opened.

The attachment blocking, by default, is on, so sometimes when you click an attachment to open it, nothing happens. All you get is a yellow bar advising you that the attachment has been blocked, as shown below.

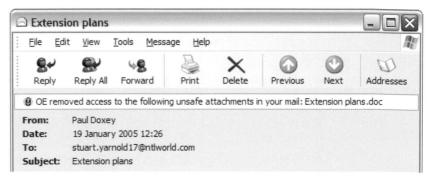

The virus protection feature is not really new. It has always been present in Outlook Express 6, but it was disabled by default until Windows XP Service Pack 1. Since then, all subsequent updates, including SP2, have turned on the feature automatically.

This is all very well and will prevent people opening dangerous attachments, either through ignorance or carelessness. However, if you think the attachment is safe – you recognize the sender, for example, you need to know how to disable it.

Before we show you how to do it though, in the interests of security, we will show you how to recognize whether or not an attachment is potentially dangerous. To do it you need to look at the file extension of the attachment.

The following is an example:

Click the message in Outlook Express and find the paperclip symbol in the lower window

Outlook Express (SP1 and SP2) can be configured to read all email in plain text format. When you enable this setting no dangerous content in the email is run. Do it as follows:

1) Start Outlook Express, and on the Tools menu, click Options

2) Click the Read tab and then tick the "Read all messages in plain text" check box under "Reading Messages"

3) Click OK

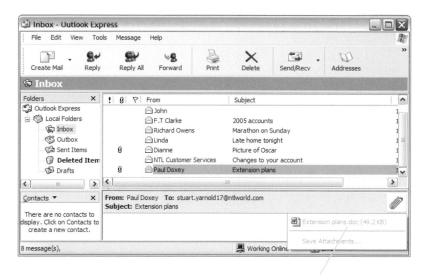

2   Click the paperclip and the file's extension will now be revealed (.doc, in our example)

Now refer to the tables on pages 156–57. These will show you which file extensions are safe to open and which are not. Once you are confident the file is safe to open, do the following:

From Outlook Express's Tools menu, click Options. Then click the Security tab

A quick method of temporarily unblocking an attachment is to simply click the Forward button (CTRL+R on the keyboard) on Outlook Express's menu bar.

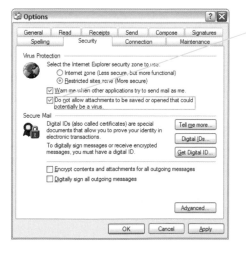

2   Uncheck the "Do not allow attachments to be saved or opened that could potentially be a virus" check box under Virus Protection, and then click OK. Now you will be able to open the attachment

High-Risk File Types

An email attachment ending in any of the file extensions in the table below can, potentially, be carrying a virus.

The list of high-risk file extensions shown on this page and page 157 is by no means exhaustive. There are many more file types that can be used to transmit a virus. However, the extensions listed here are the ones most likely to be carrying a virus.

In an effort to disguise the extension of the file in which the virus is hidden, many virus writers give the file two extensions. An example of this is the "I love you" virus which was named "LOVE-LETTER-FOR-YOU.txt.vbs". The .txt extension is harmless; the dangerous one is always the last, in this case .vbs.

If you ever get such an attachment, delete it immediately.

File Extension	Description
.ADE	Microsoft Access Project extension
.ADP	Microsoft Access Project
.BAS	Visual Basic Class module
.BAT	Batch file
.CHM	Compiled HTML help file
.CMD	Windows NT Command Script
.COM	MS-DOS application
.CPL	Control Panel extension
.CRT	Security certificate
.EXE	Application
.HLP	Windows help file
.HTA	HTML application
.INF	Setup information file
.INS	Internet communication settings
.ISP	Internet communication settings
.JS	JScript file
.JSE	JScript Encoded Script file
.LNK	Shortcut
.MDB	Microsoft Access application
.MDE	Microsoft Access MDE database
.MSC	Microsoft Common Console document
.MSI	Windows installer package
.MSP	Windows installer patch
.MST	Visual Test Source file
.PCD	Photo CD image
.PIF	Shortcut to MS-DOS program
.REG	Registry file

Be especially wary of opening attachments ending with .zip. A zip file is basically a folder, the contents of which have been compressed to reduce the size of the file.

Anyone who is familiar with computers will recognize this format and will see no inherent threat from it.

Because of this, and also the fact that XP has native support for zipped files, virus writers are increasingly using this format to package their viruses. Furthermore, many anti-virus programs have difficulty reading the contents of a zipped folder.

As an illustration of this, the Mydoom email worm was hidden in a zipped file.

.SCR	Screensaver
.SCT	Windows Script Component
.SHS	Shell Scrap Object
.URL	Internet shortcut
.VB	VBScript file
.VBE	VBScript Encoded Script file
.VBS	VBScript Script file
.WSC	Windows Script Component
.WSF	Windows Script file
.WSH	Windows Scripting Host Settings file
.ZIP	Zipped folder

Low-Risk File Types

The file types in this table are extremely unlikely to be carrying a virus and can be considered to be safe.

Two other attachment extensions to be particularly wary of are:

1) .vbs – Microsoft Visual Basic Script (VBScript). This allows the writing of scripts which have almost the same capability as executables (.exe). This includes the ability to erase or modify files on a hard drive. It can also run other programs

2) .pif – Program Information File. These files are used by Windows to run DOS programs. Since a PIF file is executable in Windows, once a person double-clicks on one of these files, it activates the virus and the trouble starts

File Extension	Description
.GIF	Picture – Graphics Interchange Format
.JPG or JPEG	Picture – Joint Photographic Expert Group
.TIF or TIFF	Picture – Tagged Image File Format
.MPEG	Movie – Motion Picture Expert Group
.AVI	Movie – Audio Video Interleaved
.MP3	Sound – MPEG compressed audio
.WAV	Sound – Audio
.TXT or TEXT	Notepad document
.BMP	Picture – Windows Bitmap
.ICO	Picture – Icon
.PNG	Picture – Portable Network Graphic
.WMF	Picture – Windows Meta File
.LOG	Log file

How to Confirm Your Message Has Been Received

If you ever send a really important email and would like to be sure that it has been received and read, you can request a Read Receipt for it.

Do this as follows:

Don't forget to deselect the Request Read Receipt option when you have sent your message. You should only use this for important messages. Constant read receipt requests will be very irritating for those at the receiving end.

1 From the Tools menu, select Options. Then click the Receipts tab

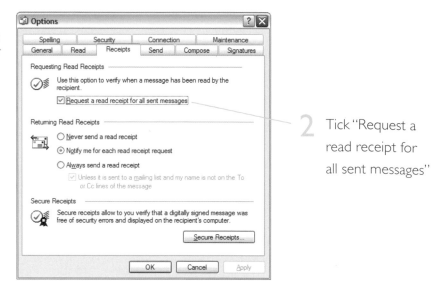

2 Tick "Request a read receipt for all sent messages"

3 When the recipient receives the message, he or she will be asked to send a receipt

While the recipient is under no obligation to send a receipt, if they do, you can rest assured that your important message has arrived.

Automatically Resize Email Pictures

As most people who regularly use email will know, Outlook Express allows users to either insert images directly into the email or attach them as a file. The commands for these actions are on the Insert menu.

Images attached in this way will be reduced in size by approximately 50%.

The problem with this is that unless the pictures have already been reduced in size in an imaging program (a process of which many people are unsure), you can end up sending an email which will take ages for the recipient to receive. Most people find this extremely irritating.

XP comes to the rescue with its email image resizing feature. Use it as follows:

1 Right-click the image you want to send with your email, select Send to and then Mail Recipient

Available for download from the Microsoft website is an Image Resizer Powertoy. This allows the resizing of a picture or group of pictures without changing the originals. It works in a similar fashion to the email image resizing feature described on this page, and can be used for the same purpose. It offers more sizing options and also allows the resizing of multiple images at the same time.

2 Select Make all my pictures smaller

3 Choose the required size

Click OK and an email message window will open with the resized image attached. All you have to do now is type in your text and press the Send button.

How to Beat the Spammers

Once you are on the spammers lists, the only way of stopping them completely is to close the account.

Spam accounts for well over half of all email traffic worldwide. That adds up to several billion every year. Furthermore, the percentage is increasing at a remorseless rate.

If you find yourself the recipient of an endless stream of advertisements, too-good-to-be-true offers, etc., what can you do about it?

The first thing is to delete your account and then set up a new one; virtually all ISPs will allow you to have several accounts. Having done this, you then need to make sure the new account is kept out of the spammers' reach. Observing the following rules will help:

Chatrooms, Newsgroups and Message Boards are favorite places for spammers. Never post your address on these sites.

1) Make your address as long as possible. Amongst other things, spammers use automated generators that churn out millions of combinations (aa@aol.com, ab@aol.com, etc.). It won't take long for them to catch up with bob@aol.com.

2) Never post your address on a website. Spammers use spiders which trawl the web looking for the @ symbol, which is in all email addresses. If you must give an address for some reason, enter it as "bob at aol.com." This will be invisible to the spiders.

3) If you need to give an address to access a specific page, give a false one. Alternatively, setup a specific account with filters that direct all received emails to the deleted items folder. Use this account when an address is asked for.

Never reply to a spammer. If you do, you are confirming that you are a real person. This makes your address valuable, and so it will invariably be sold to other spammers.

4) Never, ever, click the "Unsubscribe from this mailing list" link in a received email. This tells the spammer that your address is real and could open the floodgates.

5) Make use of your email program's filters (message rules in Outlook Express – see page 161). Properly configured, these can cut out a lot of spam.

6) Sell the PC and go and live on a desert island. It's probably the only way guaranteed to avoid spam.

Message rules are useful for purposes other than blocking spam. For example, a sales manager with a team of salesmen on the road can create a folder for all emails from his team. Inside the folder he can create further folders, one for each salesman. He can then create a set of rules that places emails from Paul into Paul's folder and emails from Sally into Sally's folder, etc.

Message rules provide an extremely effective way of managing email.

Outlook Express provides two utilities which, while not eradicating spam completely, will stop a good proportion of it.

Message Rules

Also known as filters, message rules give the user a great deal of control over what makes it into the Inbox.

For example, the table below lists just some of the options provided by Outlook Express's message rules utility.

Conditions	Actions
Specific words in the message	Delete the message
Messages from specified accounts	Do not download from the server
Messages over a specified size	Delete from the server
Messages that contain attachments	Move to a specified folder
All messages	Reply with a message

You need to be careful when creating rules to block emails. For example, if you create a rule to delete all messages containing specific words, a legitimate message that happens to contain one of those words will also be deleted. Rather than use single words, specify phrases.

Message rules can be accessed from Tools on the menu bar of Outlook Express.

Blocked Senders List

This is a simple utility that is useful for blocking persistent emails from websites or an individual. To use it, open a message from the

The Blocked Senders utility is useful for blocking emails from specific websites or individuals. Spammers constantly change their address, which makes the Blocked Senders utility less effective.

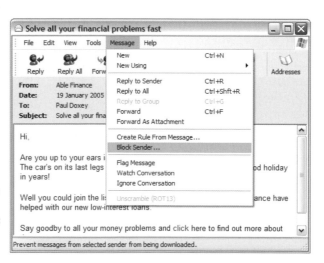

sender in question, click Message on the toolbar and then click Block Sender. From now on Outlook Express will automatically delete all subsequent emails from the sender.

Check Your Emails From Any PC

With an IMAP account, you can access and download your emails from anywhere in the world. Furthermore, as all your messages are permanently stored on the server, there is always a copy available should you lose a downloaded email.

Most email accounts are configured to use the POP3 email protocol that will download emails to the user's computer from the server. Unless specified in the email program, a copy is not kept on the server. This means that these emails can only be viewed on the user's computer.

There is, however, another email protocol available to users. This is called IMAP, and its big advantage is that all emails are stored permanently on the server. This allows them to be accessed from any PC, anywhere in the world.

Set up an IMAP account as follows:

The disadvantage of an IMAP account is that the user has to connect to the Internet to view his or her emails, unless they have already been downloaded to the computer. With an "always-on" broadband connection, this is no problem. However, dial-up users might find it inconvenient.

1   In Outlook Express, go to Tools, Accounts. Click the Mail tab, click Add and finally Mail. This opens the Internet Connection Wizard

2   The first two steps ask you to enter your name and email address respectively. The third step will ask you which email protocol you want to use

There is nothing to prevent a user from using both POP3 and IMAP with the same account. Simply setup the account with POP3 in the incoming mail server box (step 3 opposite), and then do it again with IMAP. Keep all other settings the same. This setup gives the user the advantages of both; offline reading with POP3 and universal access with IMAP.

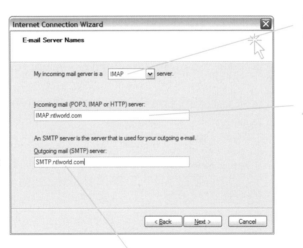

3   Select IMAP for your incoming mail server

4   In the Incoming mail server box, type IMAP, followed by your ISP's address

5   In the Outgoing mail server box, type SMTP followed by your ISP's address

6   Click Next, enter your password and then click Finish

Minimize Outlook to the System Tray

This is a very popular tip which, unfortunately, is only available to users of Outlook. It allows the user to minimize Outlook to the system tray (Notification area) rather than to the Taskbar.

Do this as follows:

Why would anyone want to do this? Well, many people use their email program constantly and not just for email. Very often email programs are used as much for their Personal Organizer features (calendars, address books, etc). Being able to minimize it to the system tray where it is out of the way but easily accessible can be very useful.

1 Open the Registry Editor and locate the following key: HKEY_CURRENT_USER\Software\Microsoft\Office\11.0\Outlook\Preferences

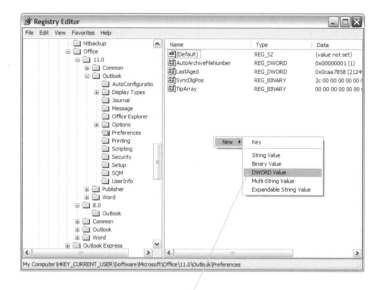

Minimizing Outlook Express to the system tray does, unfortunately, require the use of a third-party program. These are readily available from the Internet.

2 Click the Preferences folder, and on the right-hand side, right-click and create a new DWORD value. Name this MinToTray

3 Double-click MinToTray and set a value of 1

4 Close the Registry Editor and restart Windows. Open Outlook and click the minimize button. It will now minimize to the notification area

Outlook Express Keyboard Shortcuts

Here are some handy keyboard shortcuts for Outlook Express.

As with many PC applications, using the keyboard with Outlook Express can be quicker than using the mouse. The most useful of these keys are:

- CTRL+M (send & receive)
- CTRL+D (delete)
- CTRL+N (open new message)
- CTRL+I (go to Inbox)
- CTRL+O (open a folder)
- ESC (close a message)

Key	Action
F1	Open help
CTRL+A	Select all messages
CTRL+P	Print the selected messages
CTRL+M	Send and receive email
CTRL+D	Delete
CTRL+N	Open a new message
CTRL+SHIFT+B	Open the address book
CTRL+R	Reply to message author
CTRL+F	Forward a message
CTRL+SHIFT+R	Reply to all
CTRL+I	Go to Inbox
ALT+ENTER	View properties of a selected message
F5	Refresh news headers and messages
CTRL+Y	Go to a folder
CTRL+O	Open a selected message
CTRL+ENTER	Mark a message as read
CTRL+SHIFT+A	Mark all news messages as read
CTRL+W	Go to a newsgroup
CTRL+J	Go to next unread newsgroup
CTRL+SHIFT+M	Download news for offline reading
ESC	Close a message
F3	Find text
CTRL+SHIFT+F	Find a message
CTRL+TAB	Switch between Edit, Source and Preview tabs
CTRL+K and F7	Check names and spelling
CTRL+SHIFT+S	Insert signature
CTRL+> and CTRL+<	Go to next and previous message in the list
LEFT ARROW and RIGHT ARROW	Expand or collapse a news conversation

Miscellaneous

This chapter contains a general selection of tips.

Covers

Chapter Twelve

Stop XP Asking for the Installation Disk

Most people will, at some time or other, be in the process of installing an application only to see a message suddenly pop up asking them to insert the Windows CD in the CD-ROM drive.

The i386 folder is some 486MB in size. If you don't have too much hard drive space, then maybe you should think twice before using this tip.

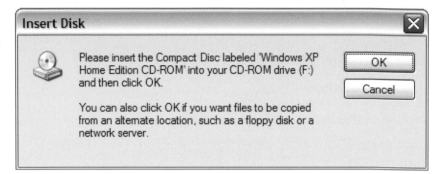

This happens because certain files have to be copied from the Windows installation disk for the application in question to work.

To prevent this happening, do the following:

1   Place the XP installation CD into the CD-ROM drive. Go to My Computer, right-click the CD-ROM drive icon and then click Open. This will reveal the contents of the CD

When it needs certain files, XP will, by default, go to the CD-ROM drive and look for the installation CD. By amending the Registry, we are telling it to look elsewhere (the i386 folder on your hard drive).

2   Find the i386 folder; right-click it and copy it to the hard drive

Next, you need to edit the Registry so that the system can find the files you have just transferred to your hard drive:

3   Open the Registry Editor and locate the following key: HKEY_LOCAL_MACHINE\Software\Microsoft\WindowsNT\ CurrentVersion

4 Click the CurrentVersion folder

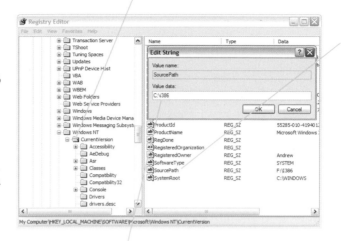

A further advantage of copying the i386 folder to your hard drive is that (should you ever need to), you can reinstall XP without the installation disk. Just open the folder and locate the WINNT32. exe file; click it and away you go.

5 Double-click Source-Path

6 In the Value data box alter the current entry to read C:\i386 (C being your hard drive). Click OK

7 Now find the registry entry at:
HKEY_LOCAL_MACHINE\Software\Microsoft\Windows\
CurrentVersion\Setup

When you have completed step 9, reboot the PC. From now on you will never be asked for the installation disk again.

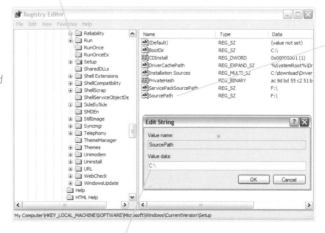

8 Click the Setup folder and then double-click Source-Path

9 In the Value data box, change the current setting to read C:\

Keyboard Calculator

Here is a handy tip which enables you to operate XP's calculator without having to bother with the mouse.

Don't forget that XP's calculator can be expanded to a scientific calculator. This option is available from the Menu bar under View.

1 Press the Num Lock key on the keyboard

2 Open XP's calculator by going to Start, All Programs, Accessories, Calculator (you can also type calc in the Run application available from the Start menu)

While the calculator supplied by Windows is perfectly adequate for most needs, there is a range of far superior and specialized calculators available for download from the Internet.

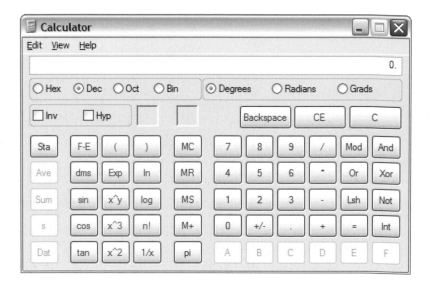

Before you can use the numeric keypad on the keyboard, the Num Lock key must be activated.

3 Instead of fiddling about with the mouse to enter numbers, simply use the numeric keypad on the keyboard

Key	Action
/	The equivalent of divide
*	The equivalent of multiply
+	The equivalent of plus
-	The equivalent of minus
Enter	The equivalent of =

Successful Minesweeping

Heres another Minesweeper cheat that will enable you to win the game with ease. When setting up a Custom game, simply set the field size to a width of 24 and a height of 30. Then set the amount of mines to 10. One or two clicks and the game's won.

Here is a tip for those of you who always like to win and which will enable you to amaze your friends.

1 Open a new game of Minesweeper

2 Click anywhere on the title bar and then type xyzzy on your keyboard. Press Shift and Enter

3 At the top left-hand corner of the Desktop you will now see a single white pixel (you'll have to look hard to see it)

The next time you play a game of FreeCell, go to Select Game in the Game menu. It will tell you to enter a number from 1 to 32000. Type "-1" or "-2." It will be like no other game of FreeCell you've played before.

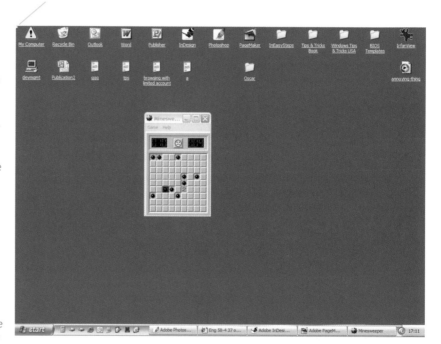

Another FreeCell cheat. While playing, press CTRL+SHIFT +F10. You will be asked if you want to Abort, Retry or Ignore. Choose ABORT, then move any card and you'll win immediately.

4 As you move the mouse cursor over the game blocks, the pixel will disappear when placed over a block containing a bomb. That's all there is to it

Compress Files and Folders with XP

Another way to use XP's compression feature is to create a zipped folder and then simply drag your files and drop them in the folder where they will be automatically compressed.

Many people like to keep their hard drive as free as possible, and one way to achieve this is by what's known as file compression.

To compress a file or folder you need a compression program that will not only compress the file, but will also decompress it when it's opened.

There are several of these on the market (a popular one is WinZip, available from most download sites).

However, unlike previous versions of Windows, XP saves you the bother as it comes with a file compression utility of its own. Use it as follows:

A very useful way of employing file compression is the creation of backup folders of important data. Ideally, these will be placed on a separate drive. Alternatively, you can use compression to store little-used files that you might otherwise delete in order to reclaim the disk space.

1 Right-click the file to be compressed

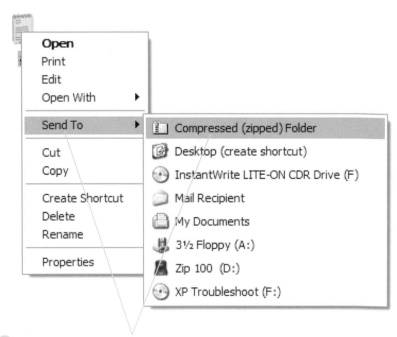

Compression is most effective when used with text-based files, and can achieve compression rates of 50% or more. Graphics files, on the other hand, might only be reduced by about 10%.

2 Select "Send To," and "Compressed (zipped) Folder"

3 Your file will now be copied, compressed and placed in a zipped folder. The original file will still be available in its uncompressed state

How to Silence the Modem

This tip only applies to those of you with an internal modem. If you have an external model then you will be able to turn down the volume manually.

Dial-up modems have an irritating way of announcing themselves when activated. This manifests itself in the form of what can be best described as a series of strangulated buzzes, clicks and whirrs.

If you are one of those types with strange nocturnal habits (browsing the Internet in the early hours when normal people are tucked up in bed), it can also be a nuisance.

So, you'll be glad to know that there is a way to shut it up.

1 Go to Start, Control Panel, Phone and Modem Options

If you click the Modem tab in step 2, you will see a speaker volume slider. If your modem has an integrated speaker, this will silence it. However, if the modem uses the system case speaker (as many do), it will be ineffective. In this case, use the ATM0 command.

2 Click the Modem tab, Properties, and the Advanced tab

3 In the Extra initialization commands box, type ATM0 (note that the last character is a zero and not the letter O)

The next time you initiate an Internet connection, the modem will be as quiet as a mouse.

How to Locate XP's Backup Utility

Previous versions of Windows have all come with an inbuilt Backup utility, as does XP Professional. Try looking for one in XP Home Edition, though, and you won't find it. This is for the simple reason that it just isn't there.

However, you may remember that in a previous tip it was recommended that you make a point of examining the contents of installation disks because of the chance of unearthing some programs that aren't installed by default.

Well, XP's Backup utility proves the point.

1 Place the XP installation disk in the CD-ROM drive and then go to My Computer. Right-click the drive and then click Open. This will display the contents of the CD

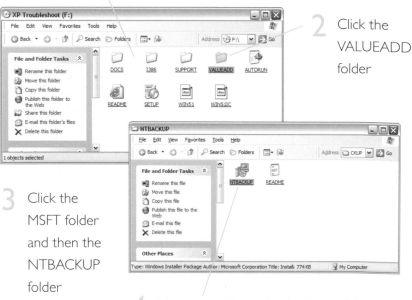

2 Click the VALUEADD folder

3 Click the MSFT folder and then the NTBACKUP folder

4 Now you will see the Backup utilities Setup file. Just click to execute it. XP's Backup application will now be available from Start, All Programs, Accessories, System Tools

Be On Time with XP

The clock in your computer is powered in exactly the same way as the majority of clocks and watches are these days – with batteries.

The batteries used in computers are usually of a high quality and will keep good time over a period of two to three years. Eventually, however, they will begin to degrade and the clock will start to lose time. While it's no big deal to reset it, XP has made it even easier with its Internet Time Synchronization feature.

This little gem is hidden away in the depths of the Control Panel in the Date and Time applet.

1 Open Date and Time, and then click the Internet Time tab

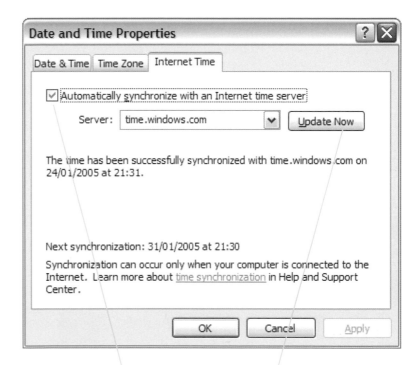

2 Tick here for Automatic Synchronization. This will occur once a week

3 Log on to the Internet and click Update Now to manually reset your system clock

Windows Update Catalog

Users who like to keep their version of XP up-to-date will be familiar with the Windows Update site. From here it is possible to download patches, updated versions of Microsoft applications (Internet Explorer, DirectX, etc), and hardware drivers.

Only users of XP and Windows 2000 will be able to access the Windows Catalog site. You must also be logged on as an administrative user.

The problem with this for users of ME and earlier Windows versions, is that downloads obtained in this way are automatically installed for them. It isn't possible to save them as a file and then install them manually as and when required. This can be a major irritation should, for example, it ever be necessary to reformat the drive and then reinstall Windows. The updates will be lost and thus must be downloaded again, a process which can take a long time, particularly if you are using a dial-up modem.

XP users are spared this annoyance as they have access to XP's version of Windows Update, which is known as the Windows Update Catalog.

1 Logon to the Internet and go to: http://v4.windowsupdate. microsoft.com/catalog/en/default.asp

Don't confuse the Windows Update Catalog with the Windows Catalog. The latter is a Microsoft website that lets you search for third-party hardware and software that is compatible with Windows XP, and compliant with the Designed for Windows XP Logo Program.

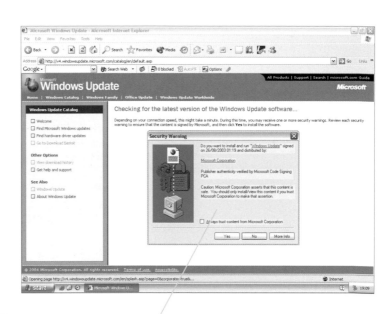

2 If this is your first visit to this site, you will be asked to install and run Windows Update. Click Yes

3 When Windows Update has been installed, locate the required updates by using the menu on the left-hand side of the page

You can find device drivers certified for use with XP in the Update Catalog by clicking Find hardware driver updates in the left-hand menu. This opens the Driver Updates page showing the different categories of device drivers available.

4 Choose the updates you want by clicking Add and then clicking Go to Download Basket

The Windows Update Catalog provides a means of saving updates as files, which can be installed as often as necessary. These can be stored on a backup medium of your choice. Having downloaded them once, you'll never need to do it again.

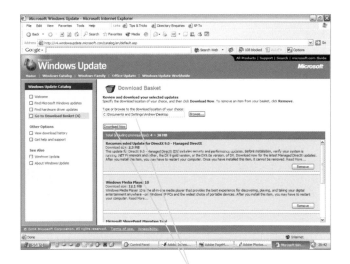

5 Browse to where you want the updates to be saved and then click the Download Now button

How to Fax with XP

XP's fax utility can only be used with a dial-up connection. Broadband users will need to use an Internet-based fax service, such as EFAX or FAXAWAY.

Just one of the many new features to be found in XP is the Fax Console. However, it isn't installed by default, so if you want to give it a try, you will have to manually install it from the XP CD. Do this as follows:

1 Place the XP CD in the CD-ROM drive

2 Go to Control Panel, Add or Remove Programs. At the left of the dialog box click Add/Remove Windows Components

There are a number of advantages to using a computer based fax system; the main one being no wasted paper. You can read, save, delete, or attach faxes to email – all without using a single piece of paper.

3 Tick the Fax Services box to install the Fax Console. Access it via Start, All Programs, Accessories, Communications and Fax

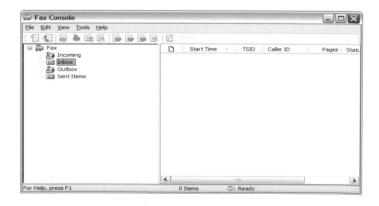

How to Restart Windows Explorer

The Task Manager is a much overlooked feature of Windows XP.

Apart from showing all the applications currently open on the computer, it also shows all the background processes running. The amount of system memory each process is using is also displayed.

This can be extremely instructive in a situation where the PC is obviously struggling to cope with the demands being made of it. By highlighting an application which is using more than its share of memory and clicking "End Process," that application can be quickly and easily closed.

From time to time, Windows Explorer, which is the application responsible for the Taskbar, Desktop and Start menu, will crash. The result is that the Taskbar and all the Desktop icons will disappear leaving a blank screen. When this happens there is little a user can do as there is nothing to click (apart from pressing CTRl+ALT+DEL to open the Task Manager. From the Task Manager's Shutdown menu, the PC can be restarted).

However, there is a better way to recover from this that doesn't involve restarting the computer. The next time Windows Explorer crashes, do the following.

1 Press CTRL+ALT+DEL to open the Task Manager

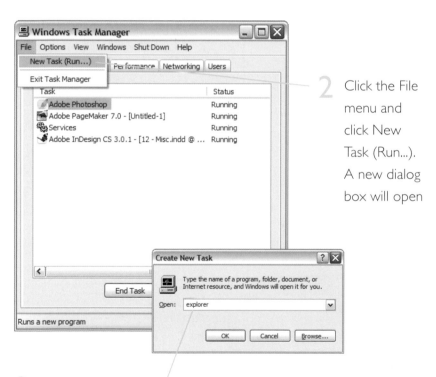

2 Click the File menu and click New Task (Run...). A new dialog box will open

Another way of opening the Task Manager is to simply right-click the Taskbar and then click Task Manager.

3 In the Open box, type explorer and then click OK

XP will now restart Windows Explorer, which will in turn, re-instate the Taskbar, Start menu, and the Desktop icons.

Quick Internet Searching

Type the word "tiger" in a search engine box and you will get millions of pages to search. These will range from the Tiger Lily restaurant in Shanghai, Tiger Woods the golfer to, not surprisingly, pages about tigers. Finding something specific will take a long time.

To help users narrow their searches, all the major search engines offer an "Advanced Search." Here you will find various options, such as specific language searches and searches restricted to pages updated within a specific time-frame, etc.

We don't have room here to list all the options provided by search engines. It must also be pointed out that different search engines work in different ways. For example, with some, the + symbol is on by default, while with others it isn't.

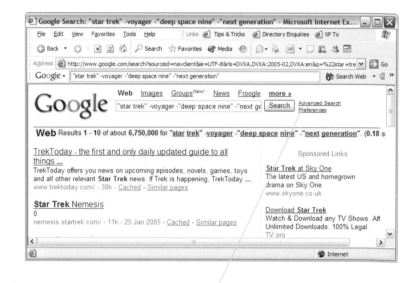

Advanced Search Options in Google

A "Search Site" feature found in the Google Toolbar (http://toolbar.google.com) allows a user to search within a specific site, even if the site does not provide a search engine of its own.

However, before you try these, the following simple tips may be all you need.

Using the + Operator

Most search engines exclude common words such as "and" and "to" and certain single digits and letters. If you want to make sure a common word is included in the search, type + before it. For example:

world war +I (make sure there is a space between the + and the previous word).

You may, at some stage, come across the phrase "Boolean Operators" with regard search engines. These are derived from Boolean Logic, which is a system for establishing relationships between terms. The three main Boolean operators are:

- *OR*
- *AND (equivalent to +)*
- *NOT (equivalent to -)*

The most useful operators are - (NOT) and quotation marks (phrase searching). These two operators can whittle a search down to literally a few hundred pages that would otherwise be several million.

Don't forget to take a look at the search engine's "Advanced Search" option as well.

Using the - Operator

The - operator allows you to exclude words from a search. For example, if you are looking for window manufacturers, type:

windows -microsoft -xp -me -98 -2000 -nt -95

This will eliminate millions of pages devoted to the various Windows operating system.

Phrase Searches

By enclosing your keywords in quotation marks, you will do a phrase search. This will return pages with all the keywords in the order entered. For example, "atlanta falcons" will return pages mainly concerning the Atlanta NFL team. Most pages regarding Atlanta or Falcons will be excluded.

Combinations of Operators

To further narrow your searches, you can use combinations of search operators and phrase searches. Using our atlanta falcons example, typing "atlanta falcons" +nfl -olympic games -birds of prey will return one thousand pages as opposed to one and a half million pages for "atlanta falcons" (results taken from Google).

OR Searches

The OR operator allows you to search for pages that contain word A OR word B OR word C, etc. For example, for a search on camping trips in either Yosemite or Yellowstone national parks, you would type the following:

"camping trips" yosemite OR yellowstone

Numrange Searches

Numrange searches can be used to ensure that search results contain numbers within a specified range. You can conduct a numrange search by specifying two numbers, separated by two periods with no spaces.

For example, you would search for computers in the $600 to $900 price bracket by typing: computers $600..900

Numrange can be used for all types of units (monetary, weight, measurement, etc).

XP's PowerToys

PowerToys are a set of handy applications that are available for download from the Microsoft website. They can also be found on many other websites. There are different versions available for the various incarnations of Windows.

To download PowerToys, aim your browser at: www.microsoft. com/windowsxp/ pro/downloads/powertoys.asp.

The most useful of the applications is undoubtedly TweakUI. This utility enables a user to make all manner of cosmetic and system changes without having to get involved in editing the Registry.

Its basic interface is shown below:

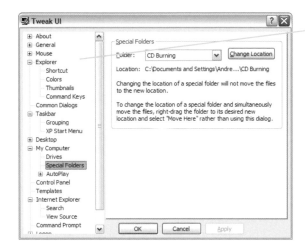

Parts of the operating system that can be modified by TweakUI

All of the PowerToys can be downloaded individually so you don't have to waste time downloading stuff you don't want. They are mostly about 500 KB in size and will take only a few minutes to download.

These are just some of the things that TweakUI can do:

- Prevent specific items appearing on the Start menu

- Remove or customize shortcut arrows

- Alter thumbnail size and resolution

- Hide drives

- Hide Control Panel applets

- Specify search engines to be used by Internet Explorer

- Hide specified user accounts on the logon screen

- Repair corrupted icons and various system folders

Automatic Email Backup for Outlook

This tip is for those of you running Outlook as your email client; unfortunately, it cannot be used with Outlook Express.

Outlook's Backup utility creates backup copies of .PST (email) files at regular intervals that are specified by the user.

To do it, you need to download a small utility from the Microsoft website, called the PF (Personal Folders) Backup. This a small 160 KB file and will download in about a minute with a dial-up connection.

Install the program and then open Outlook

If you have a separate backup medium available (a Zip drive or second hard drive), you can change the default location of the backup to this medium. This will ensure your emails cannot be lost. In the event of problems, you can restore your messages from the backup.

Open the File menu and you will see a new Backup menu item. Click this to open its options dialog box

Here, you can specify how often you want to be reminded to create a backup, and also the location of the backup folder

Improve Text Clarity

ClearType is a technology designed to smooth fonts and thus make them easier to read. Although intended primarily for LCD displays, it also makes an appreciable difference when used with a CRT monitor. Consider the two samples of text below:

ClearType has been designed to improve the legibility of text on LCD screens. However, it also significantly improves text on a CRT monitor. Give it a try – you'll never go back to using the PC without it.

The popularity of laptops are eager to use mobile XP Professional is designed computing easier. New

ClearType enabled

The popularity of laptops are eager to use mobile XP Professional is designed computing easier. New

ClearType not enabled

Enable ClearType on your system as follows:

ClearType technology uses a special technique called sub-pixel rendering to effectively triple the perceived resolution of LCD displays. When users enable ClearType, the system renders all onscreen text at three times the usual vertical resolution.

1 Open your browser and go to: www.microsoft.com/typography/cleartype/tuner/1.htm

At step 2 opposite, you will be prompted to download a ClearType tuning program. Click OK; it takes only a few seconds.

2 Tick Turn on ClearType and then click Next

Although you can enable ClearType from within XP, it is not possible to customize it. What you see is what you get. For more options you must go to the website specified in step 1 on page 182. Alternatively, the Cleartype tuning control is now available as one of Microsoft's PowerToys – see page 180.

3 Select the option that suits you best and then click Finish

To use ClearType, you must have a video adapter and monitor that support a color setting of at least 256 colors. Best results are achieved with High color (24-bit) or Highest color (32-bit) support.

Should you not have an Internet connection, you can also turn on ClearType from within Windows.

Right-click the Desktop and select Properties. Click the Appearance tab and then click Effects

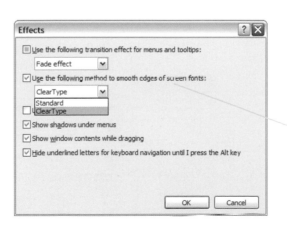

2 Tick here and select ClearType

ClearType has made a big impression and Microsoft is including it in their next release of Office (code named Office 10).

Batch Renaming of Files

Have you ever been in a situation whereby you have a whole load of related files with an assortment of meaningless or unrelated names? To make order of them you have to individually rename each file, which can be a laborious task.

Well all that is now a thing of the past. XP provides you with a means of sequentially renaming any number of files with minimum effort. You can do it as described below:

XP's batch file renaming utility is rather basic. More powerful applications of this type, offering many more features and options are available for download on the Internet.

1   Open the folder containing the files to be renamed

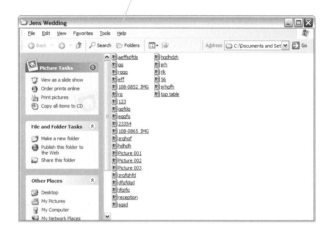

If, for any reason, you want to revert to the original file names, you can go to "Undo" in the Edit menu. This option however, will only allow you to undo a maximum of 10 files.

2   From the Edit menu on the Menu bar, click Select All. All the files will now be highlighted

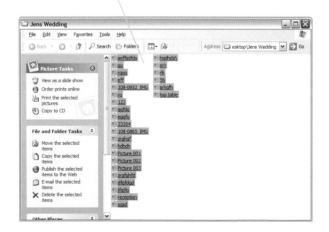

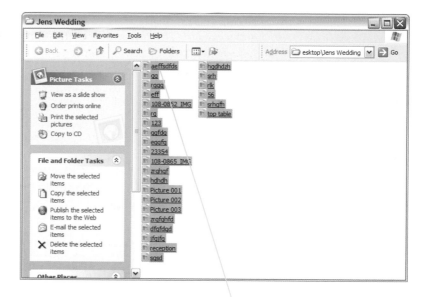

If you want to only rename some of the files in a folder, use your mouse to select the ones required and then rename the first selected file.

3 Right-click the first file in the list and click Rename. Type a suitable name and then click once anywhere in the folder. The files will now be automatically renamed

If the file extension is visibile in the rename box, be sure to include it in the new name, or you will get a warning message about changing the file type.

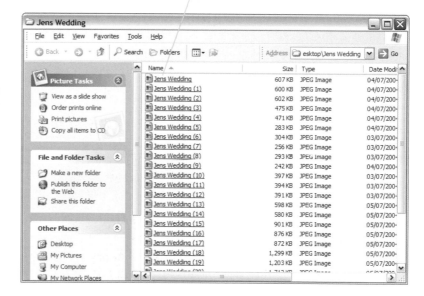

How to Test Your Connection-Speed

Tests from these sites do not measure the actual speed of your modem: what they measure is the bandwidth between your modem and the test site itself.

This is a very simple and easy method of establishing how quickly your computer is communicating with the Internet. You can do it out of curiosity, or when you are experiencing slow browsing or downloading speeds and want to see where the problem lies.
To do it, you need to visit a connection-speed test website. There are many of these sites, and most of them work by downloading a large image to your PC and measuring the time taken to do it. NOTE: these tests do not measure the speed of the modem (see top margin note).

The results from www.testmyspeed.com, using the author's Cable modem, are shown below:

Some speed test sites offer more options, such as measurement of Upload speeds and Ping tests. The latter can help you determine if poor performance is due to your computer, your connection, or Internet congestion.
A good example of this type of site is www.pcpitstop.com.

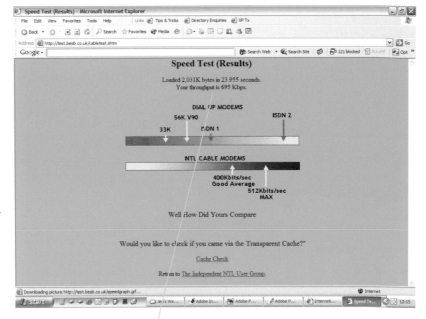

Here we can see that the 2031 KB test file downloaded in just under 24 seconds at a throughput speed of 695 Kbps

These sites can be useful in determining whether slow connections or downloads are being caused by the Internet itself, specific sites or the PC.

Index

High-definition TV 86
High-resolution video 81
Hijackers 25, 103
Hotmail 138

S

T

U